The Whole Foods Diet

Your Guide to Whole Food Shopping, Cooking, Eating & Money-Saving Recipes

Andrea Huffington

Primal Publishing

Atlanta, Georgia USA

ISBN 978-1-49965-613-8

9 781499 656138 >

Editorial reviews

"There's so much I didn't know about whole foods before reading this book. It gave me so much to learn and follow, and with amazing results. I'm proudly converted to the whole foods way of dieting!"

*****Laine G. Hand Hartford, Connecticut

"Well-explained, complete with very good, whole recipes. I give my highest commendations. If you're starting out on the whole foods diet, pick this one up. "

*****Robert A. Morse Cumberland, Maryland

"You'll find all you need to know about whole foods here. No complicated explanations, a quick read with very easy to do recipes with ingredients at the least price. Great!"

*****Jason Reed Savannah Georgia

Thank you for downloading my book. Please REVIEW this book on Amazon. I need your feedback to make the next version better. Thank you so much!

BOOKS BY ANDREA HUFFINGTON

Paleo Slow Cooker Recipes

Going Paleo on a Budget

The Easy Paleo Diet Beginner's Guide

Living Gluten-free on a Budget

Paleo Pressure Cooking!

Living Gluten-free On a Budget

Foreword

A well-figured, healthy body managed by whole, nutritious food that leaves you wanting more.

No sweet or carb compulsions, no pining for easy-on-the-eyes platefuls of sinful, yet destructive food…just clean, nutrition-packed bites that take off unnecessary fats and damaging components that may have already entered themselves into your system.

You can put a stop to these escalating risks and instead give your body the nutrition it rightfully deserves, leaving you healthier and in the best shape ever! Well-established and popular author, Andrea Huffington shares to you in her new bestseller *The Whole Foods Diet* just how well you can overcome your struggles to maintain a healthy diet and lose those disheartening pounds! Some of her best works, include *Paleo Slow Cooker Recipes, Paleo Pressure Cooking and The Easy Paleo Diet Beginner's Guide*, you may find, are ultimate must-reads for people looking to reverse their bad eating habits, go the right route, and finally achieve healthy living. Andrea Huffington is the perfect go-to person if you're looking to transform a below average eating lifestyle to awe-inspiring habits of picking healthy whole wheat food.

"The Whole Foods Diet," is a basic, yet extensive guide that teaches you the fundamentals for a successful whole foods diet. You will be able to establish a workable diet plan, arming yourself with priceless tips that will shape you on your way.

Discipline is the essential factor of a well-maintained diet. Pair it with a great book to kick-start with, and you're just a step closer to positive transformation!

TABLE OF CONTENTS

While all attempts have been made to provide effective, verifiable information in this Book, neither the Author nor Publisher assumes any responsibility for errors, inaccuracies, or omissions. Any slights of people or organizations are unintentional.

This Book is not a source of medical information, and it should not be regarded as such. This publication is designed to provide accurate and authoritative information in regard to the subject matter covered. It is sold with the understanding that the publisher is not engaged in rendering a medical service. As with any medical advice, the reader is strongly encouraged to seek professional medical advice before taking action.

Introduction

As a woman who grew up in California, food like barbeque, burgers, non-traditional pizza (fresh produce with barbequed meat ingredients), and anything influenced from Latin cuisine (tacos, tortas, quesadillas), to Asian-inspired dishes that gave birth to the California roll, I was blessed to live in a state with a bounty of always appetizing food.

In retrospect, attention to weight did not for one moment dictate my choices for meals, regardless if it had for others. I was young, I was loving life, and food was always part of that. Coming across broad selections of food remained somewhat of a little adventure to me. As I stepped toward University of California, Los Angeles (UCLA) however, the effect of others' perception concerning figure slowly began to bother me. More and more, I noticed that most girls' biggest aim was to look flawless. I would go to parties, and almost (if not) all the ladies had a manner of revealing their perfectly-shaped or well-figured bodies. From mini skits, high-fashion cocktail dresses, to in-style designer frocks and coats, a sexy figure was considered something of a great asset, which much to my regret, did not have. And so all throughout my university years, as my way of avoiding the problem, I pretended that it was not a big matter that I needed to ponder on so heavily. I was still young and I did not want a set of restrictions to hinder me from enjoying everything good about life, including food. In some manner I was aware that I needed to do something about my eating habits, yet I could never forego from a lifelong routine of eating delicious treats that were not good for my body. To add to the disappointment, at this period, I had to acknowledge a disheartening discovery. I was diagnosed diabetic.

Shortly after graduation, I was given a great opportunity to practice my profession in another continent. As a woman who yearns for knowledge and new encounters, I accepted the promising offer as chemical engineer in an illustrious company in India. Living in an entirely different culture was exciting. Friendly people, fascinating discoveries…from ancient monuments, ethnic customs to unique culinary experiences, I took my life to a bold new leap.

After a time, I embraced India as a country wealthy in spice. There, I was introduced to a kind of cuisine that was unfamiliar yet pleasantly palatable. I gained high respect for the Eastern culture, the Indian fusion and passion for cuisine. Chenna gaja, paratha, mishti doi, every new alluring find was within glance. Diet was the one thing I increasingly lost control of. One day, an epiphanizing experience changed my perspective forever. The subtle reign of diabetes finally struck a hard blow. As it soared, my health plummeted. My husband was very concerned. He urged that I return home immediately and be medically attended. Back in the United States, I would receive treatment from more advanced science and technology topnotch doctors could offer, and be with loving friends and family.

At that stage in my life, I finally realized my faults, and decided to pursue a different, life-changing direction. I urged myself, "Andrea, it's time for a change." I started eating responsibly. I turned my same passion for food into a new passion for finding food that was good for me and for my family. Maintaining a proper diet was now a top priority, and poor health decisions, a thing of the past. I dabbled with mixing up selections, adding fruits and vegetables to my meals without restricting too much on the choices I loved best (cuts of ham, lamb, bacon). However, I realized, I was not adding towards improvement with that method, but I was cheating on my objectives. I decided to seek for sources online that would prove useful. I was going to really stick to my target. I tried a range of new diets. From Dukan, Alkaline, Hacker's to the South Beach Diet, they offered their own promising alternatives that inspired me to ditch my poor food choices and maintain a balanced weight. Much to my disappointment a little later, none of them were the magic mixtures that could switch my lifestyle and win over the disease. One day, a friend introduced me to the Paleolithic diet. After that, my life took a drastic turn for the better.

As an overview, Paleo diet, like others, is a promising nutritional plan. But this one is derived from the presumed dietary intake of our ancestors, the Paleolithic humans (whom we know proved to have lived healthier, more extended lives). This diet comprises mainly of food that past dwellers typically used to gather or hunt. You will find staples such as fruits, herbs, vegetables, roots, grass-fed pasture, wild game meats, seeds, spices, nuts, insects and fish, which are found to have a higher constituent of omega-3 fats, meaning better nutritional value. Eliminating legumes, grains, dairy products, refined salt and sugar, processed oils and potatoes, I learned that the Paleo diet works, and remarkably. Unlike several raw food diets, the Paleo way allowed me to cook my food. And like many of its practitioners, I maintained drinking only water or tea, restricting sodas and other sugar-packed liquids that we know are really bad for one's health.

A few months after maintaining my diet, I decided to take another step further. I began exercising. I started with a mere thirty-minute jogging three times a week, and then slowly pacing myself with four times a week at an hour and thirty minutes per session. My body gradually responded at best. My diabetes weakened, and my health has never been better. I hired a fitness coach who taught me how to build my muscles while I continued to implement the rules of my diet plan. At this point, my life embarked on a new chapter. I felt like a new person. Most of all, I learned and earned the rewards of discipline. The amazing turnout of my diet's plan gave me a brand new perspective on life. I felt much, much better about myself.

Realizing further, I felt the need to share what I learned. To tell people why healthy choices are significant and why change is so important. I wanted to send this message to everyone. That's how I began to write. I hope you realized the moral that I'm trying to impart to you as my reader. With self-discipline and persistent drive, you can fight and overcome your weaknesses and take control of your life. As an advocate of searching for better ways to practice one's lifestyle by choosing right and healthy choices, I am going to introduce you to the world of whole foods, and its wondrous benefits. I won't be expounding much about the Paleo diet (I have several works on those you can check), because among the many researches I have done, the whole foods diet was one of those that I found very promising and beneficial altogether. Here, you will be able to pick up bits and pieces of facts on whole foods, learn its essentials, and apply it in your regular diet. A nourishing regimen would include at least 70-80% whole foods in your meal.

Among the many advantages whole foods have on your body, know that fiber, vitamins, minerals, beneficial fats, and the combined nutritional value in whole food plant protect us from disease. More so, they contain antioxidants that prevent cell damage. Fresh fruits, vegetables, beans, seeds, whole grains: oats, buckwheat, quinoa, etc; legumes like lentils or chick peas; seafood: shrimp, soft shell crabs, lobster, etc; and eggs, are the good food for you. You should be looking out on these, instead of French fries, chips or donuts.

Did you know that processed foods contain more preservatives as well as additives? Not only that, they have allergens, are very high in sodium, and are jammed with artery–clogging hydrogenated oils. If you're fond of eating potato chips, candy, sugary cereals, baked products and the rest of the family, be alert that they're extremely low in fiber and super high in calories! This results in weight gain because study shows your stomach takes longer to feel a full sensation compared to when eating high-fiber whole foods. Do you really think persisting on processed foods over the healthy ones is the best choice? Perhaps my book will enlighten you otherwise. If you want to stop your bad habits now, and pursue a successful way of changing your eating habits, you can have a diet that still respects you without limiting on a variety of choices. Whether you're worried about bland flavors that may not suit your taste, are working to keep away from salts and sugars, are looking for the most helpful whole foods product recommendations to fit your budget, or want to acquire a successful whole foods meal plan, have my book beside you as a helpful guide. My book will make you rethink your choices. You will learn how great the whole foods diet can really be.

A successful diet is not a miracle that grows overnight, but neither is it unachievable. It takes time and diligence. The whole foods diet is one I would recommend to anyone who hopes to achieve a healthier way of living. This book will provide you with dozens of whole foods information and tips. I hope you can take as much as you can and apply it well. Happy reading!

Introducing Whole Foods

Before hitting off with a new diet plan, one usually asks: Will this diet really work for me? or What restrictions are going to be hard to follow once I set out?; and maybe even: Are there things I need to prepare myself with before starting? Doubts such as these are normal to encounter and questioning on the whole foods diet is not an exclusion. So as a healthy food junkie, I did my research and narrowed down the most common dilemmas people face with prior to pursuing the whole foods diet. Thereafter, you will read the solutions I have also provided.

To give a brief definition, whole foods are those food that have not gone through any kind of alteration or processing. This means, they contain almost no additives (salt, sugar and other artificial ingredients) to make them taste extra sweet or appetizing. Whole foods are unrefined, and need not be modified, which then makes it naturally good for you. It provides you with close to 100% of the essential food nutrients based on its original nutritional value. They need not go through needless processes such as preserving, freezing, injecting, baking or roasting. Whole foods can never be canned, boxed nor jarred.

Here is a list of whole foods to get you familiarized on the basic:

- ✓ Fresh fruit
- ✓ Nuts and seeds
- ✓ Seaweed (sea vegetables)
- ✓ Raw milk
- ✓ Brown rice
- ✓ Whole grains
- ✓ Fresh vegetables
- ✓ Beans and other legumes
- ✓ Eggs
- ✓ Unprocessed meat without additives
- ✓ Organ meat without additives
- ✓ Fish and shellfish without additives

Whole Foods and its Categories

Whole foods are proven to provide complete nutritional ingredients your body needs, comparing them to the processed kind. They retain all vital and original components of fiber, protein, vitamins minerals, healthy fat, enzymes, minerals and other essential nutrients. Like all other food, whole foods have their divisions. They are: vegetables, nuts, seeds, fruits, grains and legumes. Below is a table provided for you to easily identify some whole foods that belong to their family.

Whole Fruits	Whole Vegetables	Whole Nuts and Seeds
Lemons	Carrots	Peanuts
Bananas	Squash	Walnuts
Figs	Kale	Macadamia Nuts
Peaches	Dandelion Greens	Pistachio
Mangoes	Eggplant	Almonds
Grapes	Artichokes	Cashews
Pineapples	Yams	Hazelnuts
Honeydew	Broccoli	Sesame
Kiwis	Cucumber	Pumpkin
Tomatoes	Fresh Beans	Sunflower
Clementines	Brussel Sprouts	Linseeds

Whole Grains	Whole Legumes
Brown Ride	Chickpeas
Corn	Split Peas
Cornmeal	Lima Beans
Wheat	Kidney Beans
Rye	Black Beans
Amaranth	Soya Beans
Rolled Oats	Lentils
Oat Groats	Lupini Beans
Millet	Pinto Beans
Popcorn	Red Beans
Hulled Barley	Flageolet Beans

Replacing your current snack diet with whole foods such as legumes, will give you high protein amounts with little to no fat. Other alternatives are nuts and seeds, which aren't artificially flavored. You don't have to worry about food processing, as whole foods allow us to take in whole nutritional values. There are so many health benefits if you include whole foods as part of your diet. Whole grain foods especially help lessen the risk of chronic diseases such as obesity, stroke, obesity, coronary heart diseases and diabetes.

Did you know that whole foods such as fiber help your body process sugar without heightening your insulin? Aside from suppressing your taste that prevents you from eating sweets that spoil your appetite for real food, taking in whole foods naturally fill up your hunger without you having to worry about overeating. A whole foods diet can give you more nutrition compared to the totality of an individual serving of food. Also, the whole foods taste is distinct, revealing the central nutrients inside it.

Whole Grains

Regardless of what others may believe, whole grains do not actually make you gain weight; the real culprit is refined carbohydrates which are found in donuts, cookies, cakes, and many other forms of bread. Whole grains are filled with antioxidants, fiber, B vitamins, minerals, protein, and trace minerals (iron, copper, magnesium and zinc. They still offer a sweet taste. The best thing about them is, whole grains sustain your energy. So even if your entire day was used up doing vigorous activities, you'll less likely to get tired quickly compared to eating the average food to start your day.

Did you know eating whole grains slows down your stomach's digestion? This allows your body to get more out of the nutrients it needs from food. So try switching your usual bread diet to whole grain bread instead. Instead of white, have some brown rice, or make pasta using whole wheat brands. If you're used to Saltines, why not go for whole grain crackers as an alternative?

Here is a list of whole grain foods you can add for a perfect whole foods diet:

- Brown rice
- Bulgur(cracked wheat)
- Bulgur Mille
- Buckwheat
- Popcorn (no salt or butter)
- Quinoa
- Sorghum
- Triticale
- Wild rice
- Whole rye
- Whole-grain barley
- 100% Whole-grain bread (e.g. bagels, English muffins, Pita bread)
- Whole-grain chips and snacks (e.g. baked tortillas, granola bars, corn chips)
- Whole-grain corn
- Whole-grain pasta (e.g. corn, amaranth, quinoa)
- Whole oats/oatmeal
- Whole-grain cereals (e.g. rolled oats, buckwheat, cheerios, toasted oat cereal)
- Whole-grain flour (e.g. whole rye flour, millet, spelt flour)
- Whole wheat

What can you say about whole grains? Don't they sound good to eat?

Why Whole Foods?

"What are in whole foods?" "Why is it the diet plan to go to?" "Can you give me examples of the whole foods that I can eat?" This is the section of the book where I will discuss to you prevalent questions that pop in your head, providing you a clear breakdown on all there is to know about whole foods and why they're good for you. By the end of this book, you will be able to absorb the basic must-knows on whole foods, so you can take the first step to a successful whole foods budget diet and shed those pounds off!

With whole foods, you have all the liberty in acquiring most of the original nutrients food offers. No processing, no inessential cancer or heart disease contributors. I made some bullet points below if you need more facts to convince you on why whole foods are best for your body.

Absorption- When food is whole; more nutrients are able to synergize themselves inside your body. For example, drinking whole versus low fat or skim milk may prohibit you from taking in the fat soluble ingredients. And our bodies require fat to assimilate fat-soluble vitamins. So why not go skim?

Avoid Needless Additives - Do you ever notice the nutrition labels on packaged food products? There are instances when you see chemical ingredients or numbers you're not familiar with? It's best you stay away from these because these hard-to-identify ingredients may contain hidden menaces, unnecessary doses of refined sugar, salt, fat or flour.

Complex Carbohydrates – Whole foods such as whole grains are crammed with complex carbohydrates. Because food manufacturers mill grains, refined grains lack the nutrients its original state provides, thus digesting itself inversely in your body. It's now more of simple carbohydrates, missing most nutritional values.

Fiber – If you didn't know yet, fiber helps slow down sugar absorption of food such as whole grains, fruits or vegetables. It breaks sugar release of whole grains and insulin. That is why, if you choose to eat refined food such as white flour that are low in fiber, you may not be getting most of the nutrition you need, and will have a tendency to grab for more food on the table.

Larger Nutrient Amounts Per Calorie –Vitamins and macro nutrients have lesser calories and more nutrition compared to processed food coated with unhealthy fats and white sugar. When you eat whole foods on the other hand, you're more able to consume your daily count for vitamins, minerals, and other macro nutrients. This is good especially if you're looking out for the calories you consume.

Nutrients- Like fiber, there are plenty other nutrients in food that we seem to disregard. The more processed products you consume. Remember that you would always lack vital nutrients such as fiber if you consume more processed products.

Choosing the whole foods way of eating isn't as tough as you think. Everyone's overstressed or overworked, but we have to make the decisions that coincide on what resources we have set on the table.

Let's clear some more facts on whole foods:

1. Healthy food is not necessarily pricier.

According to research, choosing to buy whole and real food is not more expensive compared to when eating fast food, processed food, or junk food. In fact, the top 4 products sellable in grocery stores are all drugs: sugar, nicotine, alcohol and caffeine.

Do you really need a bottle of alcohol? Maybe you can get a carton of organic milk. When you cut out on alcohol especially, your grocery bill will go down tremendously. Think about that the next time you go shopping for the week's essentials.

2. Healthy food does not need so much time for preparation.

Unlike food loaded with carbs and fats that are pleasing to look at, with healthy food like whole foods, you do not have to spend too much time on the kitchen preparing complicated meals. Fresh and natural food is easy to prepare once you know the recipes. Later on, I'll show you.

3. Healthy food is not hard to find.

You do not have to visit a health-food store, a gourmet food store, farmer's market, or eat purely organic to be considered a healthy eater. There are plenty of healthy foods in your local supermarket. Try looking for them outside store aisles.

Now that you know the differences, do you think you can make smarter choices the next time you visit the farmer's market? Surely you're quite convinced now. Do you plan on switching your diet tomorrow?

Whole Foods and Organic Foods

Here, I will provide some brief distinctions between organic food and whole foods because these two so often get mixed up. I want to clear some uncertainties because you may need this information as you go along your whole foods journey.

Whole foods, as we have covered earlier, describes food that is close to its original state edible. Whole foods do not go through processing and are free of additives, chemicals and preservatives, thereby giving you the complete package of nutrition your body really craves for.

Organic food on the other hand, is food such as meat, poultry, and dairy from animals that have not been fed or injected with growth hormones or antibiotics for fattening and protection. They haven't been processed, yet their meat has been played when they were alive. Organic fruits and vegetables are the same thing, except they haven't been bioengineered, sprinkled with pesticide or radiated. Organic food is cultivated through animal and environment-friendly methods of farming.

Whole Foods vs. Synthetic Supplements

Here, I will inform you of the differences between vitamins and whole food supplements. Despite what vitamins and minerals tablets say they alternatively offer, it is not possible for you to get the same nutritional value when eating real food. The negative side to supplements is they only give you one nutrient you are missing. You cannot get the same quantity and quality of vitamins you're taking in. In fact, vitamins from United States Pharmacopoeia (USP) vitamins cannot be found in any food at all! When they say "natural" supplements, they are actually referring to drug-like chemicals that many of which come from the ground.

Moreover, synthetic supplementation can prove to be harmful to your body. It is found that heavy ascorbic acid supplementation thickens our arterial walls up to nearly 3x as much, risking one further to heart disease. Because of the lack of natural absorption, supplements stress the liver and kidneys while your body works to get rid of unneeded chemicals. Many fruits and vegetables contain a balanced range of nutritional contents that when fused, work well together, resulting in proper functioning your body needs. Synthetic supplements on the other hand are not able to provide you with the complete nutritional table that otherwise whole foods can offer. Whole foods have a quicker digestion process that allows your body to absorb all the micronutrients rather than put them to waste.

Due to the fact that our soils are depleting, containing less and less trace minerals and other vitamins, it's even more damaging to know that in today's generation, food now has a lessened nutritional value compared to 25-50 years ago. For example, iron in spinach now only contains 1.5% from 60 years back, and an orange only has one-tenth of its Vitamin C left compared to 30 years ago. This is the reason why having whole foods as your diet must be taken to action.

To give you a better comparison between whole foods and synthetic supplements, here is a table I've made. Switch from synthetic and go for whole! You will see how much more of natural nutrition you get on a daily basis.

Synthetic Supplements

Contains Vitamin B-6 (pyridoxine hydrocholine), a synthetic USP chemical

Isolated chemicals that the body cannot easily identify and use

Small absorption process, mostly excreted

High doses of Vitamin E synthetics squanders calcium and magnesium from bones

High doses of Vitamin A links to a higher risk of cancer

Take from merely one molecule out of a large one, thus lacking vital components. Vitamins A, C, D, E, beta-carotene, alpha-tocphero, and many other nutrients and minerals are designed to last a long are incomplete and do not function properly as "vitamins"

Synthetic vitamins' metabolism leads to imbalance and overdose in body chemistry

Once whole foods are taken apart through

processing or refining, it cannot be taken back together and now considered are nonfunctional

Whole Foods

No pyridoxine hydrocholine. Natural B-6

High-complex vitamins (carbs, proteins, bioflavonoids, lipids, etc.) that the body can easily identify and use

Selective absorption. Body is built for nourishment from natural food for health optimization

Sustains calcium and magnesium in bones

Natural Vitamin A (e.g. spinach) prevents cancer

Complete vitamins grouped in chemically-related compounds with micronutrients, cofactors, anti-oxidants, trace minerals and more components the body seeks

Proper functioning and distribution of vitamins

Always full and completely functional

Whole Foods for Active Individuals

Are you fond of exercising? Exercise is a good thing. But if it's all exercise, with a poor balance of nutrients, you will only be putting a great workout to waste. Weight lifting, running or using the treadmill should be paired with before and after exercise regimens so you can get the most out of your daily exercise program. Allow yourself to get the proper balance of micronutrients and macronutrients. I've provided some tips below so you can be reminded of how to take care of your body before and after every exercise session.

"Carbo" Loading

Getting to the topic on people's belief about stuffing up with carbs prior to an intense exercise is necessary. But first we have to distinguish the carbs. There are two types: refined and unrefined. To put it simply, refined carbs are bad, and unrefined carbs are good because they have not gone through a process of manufacturing. Instead of eating white bread or pasta, why not eat whole grains or fresh fruits and vegetables? They are full of fiber to keep you blood sugar balanced while giving your stomach time for unhurried digestion.

Fuel for Workout

Before every workout, between 1 to 4 hours, keep in mind to pump your body with enough unrefined carbs to stimulate your muscles. Whether it's an apple or a slice of whole wheat bread, there should be enough traces of carbohydrates and calories to fuel you for your upcoming exercise. The harder the exercise, the more intake is recommended.

Fast Muscle Recovery

It's important to know that whenever you're working out, especially when it's intense, your muscles strain and tear. Once your muscle fibers are ripped through due to overwork, its' when your muscles start to rebuild themselves. Before they do, they need some time to recover. You can tell because of the level of soreness you feel afterward. So it's always good to nourish your muscles by taking in the proper nutrition, otherwise it would take longer to heal, resulting in lesser workouts per week.

Here's how:

Within 30-45 minutes after every workout, you need to provide your body with the right food which include protein and carbohydrates. I recommend that you eat a piece of fruit immediately after doing your exercise and then you can add a heavier meal within the hour. Try a leafy salad, brown rice or sweet potato Don't feast on a steak, burger or bucket of fries. Remember, self-control. Later on, I will introduce you to a perfect plant-based whole foods diet that will aid your muscle recovery.

Consider Hydration

Dehydration is embodied by dizziness, imbalance, cramps or extreme fatigue. Nobody wants to experience this now, do they? So remember that in every exercise, water is the significant player in loosening your joints, regulating your temperature, and giving your body the nutrients it needs.

Whether it's before, during, or after your exercise, lots of water for hydration stimulation is required for the body's refueling. I would recommend drinking water every 20 minutes while exercising and even after exercising. Your body will just let you know when it's finished hydrating. Try adding a squeeze of lemon to your drink if you get tired of water after a while. Lemon does not only add flavor, but gives you extra vitamins.

Now if you're an active individual, you would need to take in more calories to supplement the energy you use up. However, this does not automatically say that athletes should keep eating concentrated protein food such as meat or eggs. Have some whole wheat pasta, beans or quinoa. I'll show you some good whole wheat foods you can substitute with.

The Ultimate Whole Foods Diet

Are you hopeful that this diet is the one that finally work for your favor? Do you believe that you can achieve your best shape through my help? Are you looking for answers that provide consistent results on whole foods? If you agree, you can now have it!

In this chapter, I will expound on the whole foods diet, how to attain your goal weight through the whole foods diet, how you can manage shifting to whole foods, as well as my nutritional recommendations for the whole foods diet. So let's begin.

What is a Whole Foods Diet?

As we've learned, "Whole Food" is one close to its original state as much possible. We've learned that food such as whole grains, nuts, fruits and vegetables have retained fiber, phytochemicals and other nutrients that processed food cannot provision. Health experts suggest that health improvement and disease prevention are better attainable when you're maintaining a whole foods-based diet. So you are about to start a diet that constitutes purely of unrefined/unprocessed ingredients. Hooray to healthy!

Because this is a strategic diet, losing weight naturally is not going to be very difficult as you initially think it could be. I will be your guide. As long as you follow my tips and advice to the letter, losing weight while staying healthy should be very easy to attain.

The first step to achieving your goal begins with self-discipline. With the whole foods weight loss plan, you are urged to control your consumption for food with refined sugar and flour, while enhancing your appetite for unprocessed food that have minimal protein, starch and fat. Whole foods eating means consuming food naturally, completely - without the nutrients meddled with. This is beneficial even for persons with high blood pressure, obesity, elevated triglycerides, or glucose intolerance.

Remember the codes when eating whole foods:
1.) Eat food packed with nutrition

2.) Make use of all the ingredient as much as possible (e.g. cartilage, potato peelings)

3.) Create and eat naturally fermented food and drink

4.) Use produce grown locally whenever you can

5.) Use vegetables taken from the sea

6.) Use biodynamic and seasonal organic produce

7.) Use grey celtic sea salt vs. table salt (mineral composition contrasts)

8.) Minimize the usage of refined sugar

9.) Consume a variation of food groups

The whole foods way of dieting gives you top essential nutrients your body yearns for. Not only are you taking in healthy daily servings, but you will lose weight faster! As you start your new diet plan, here is a table to guide you of some food I recommend you eat and stay away from.

What to eat	Instead of
Whole grains	Refined grains
Fruits, vegetables, beans	Fiber and vitamin supplements
Baked potato with chopped green onions and light sour cream	Sour cream and onion potato chips
Fresh berries in your breakfast meal	Breakfast bars or blueberry toaster pastries
Skinless chicken breast with healthy ingredients	Chicken nuggets with flavoring, preservatives and added fats
Raspberry smoothie blended with real raspberries and banana yogurt	Ice or slushy with pink coloring

With whole foods, variety is never a challenge as there are never-ending customized choices inspired from cuisines all across the world. Whole foods present your food picks as you grow a fondness for new tastes and acquire taste discernment.

Achieving a Healthy Weight through Whole Foods

If you are fast hoping to be in the weight you've always dreamed of, then you're on the right track reading my book. The whole foods diet supplies your body with the nutrients it really needs, unprocessed, with little to no unhealthy constituents. You don't have to be fixated on calorie, fat or carb counting, rather concentrate on eating what is nutritious. Eating whole foods is proven to improve your metabolism and burn your fat faster. Whole foods are also high in fiber, phytonutrients and vitamins and minerals. Instead of consuming carbohydrate-laden or sugar-packed goods, lose weight naturally and gradually diminish your appetite for sinful treats through whole foods.

After doing my research and applying it over the years, I have found that if you consume more food with fiber and other nutrition to your appetite's filling, you will be less tempted to cheat with an unhealthy, delicious snack or meal. Because the body craves for natural nutrition, it suppresses the urge to grab something from the fridge or cupboard. Be reminded that eating when you're not hungry is a bad trait and hampers your whole foods diet. So eat only when you're hungry, and eat the nutritious ones. I also highly encourage that you eat vegetarian meals. Sooner or later, your regular craving for pre-packed food turn into a craving for whole foods.

If you want to know what food and drinks you're allowed and not allowed to eat and drink, below is a small checklist you can dig into without having to worry about breaking your whole foods diet.

Sample of food and drink you can have:

✓ Salads using non-starchy vegetables

✓ Egg whites

✓ Fish

✓ Lean meat (ham, poultry, turkey bacon, reduced-fat sausages)

✓ Reduced fat cheese (e.g. cottage cheese)

✓ Low-calorie fresh fruit and veggie juices

✓ Diet soft drinks (occasionally)

✓ Drinks: water, coffee, tea

✓ Low-calorie condiments (sour pickles, Worcestershire sauce, sea salt, vinegar, etc.)

Because the whole foods diet is a low glycemic diet, it concentrates on food that takes a longer duration for digestion. As a result, it releases itself as glucose to your bloodstream. Meaning, you have to say tata to white food. White foods are labeled, "bad carbs" (the perpetrator to today's obese in America). Bad carbs refer to processed and refined food like pasta, flour, rice, bread, crackers, cereal, including simple sugars like table sugar. White food fuels insulin and carb cravings. So white rice, white bread, sugar, and the rest of this category, have to be a nono if you want to keep away from bad carb. Yogurt, skim milk, white beans, onions, turnips and cauliflower are still alternatives you can munch on.

Consider the difference between consuming highly processed and additive-filled food over food in its natural whole. Which can you say has fewer calories? The answer will always remain to be natural food. No oil, no high level of sodium, no butter, sugar or any fatty condiments. Do yourself a favor and turn a new leaf now because all processed food has ever really been doing is add to your weight, risk you of cancer, type 2 diabetes and heart disease. Eliminate these bad choices now and achieve the weight you are meant have. Sooner or later, you will be more mindful of what you put on your plate, and be alert to stay away from the hard-to-pronounce ingredients at the back of jarred and canned goods. **Start today and maintain a healthy weight! Help me show you.**

5   Easy Steps to the Whole Foods Goodness Diet

1.) Whenever you can, pick products with 100% whole grains.

2.) Eat plenty of beans, fresh fruits and vegetables in snacks and in meals.

3.) Eat less processed snacks and pre-packed goods.

4.) Drink less sugar-concocted beverages. Have water, fresh fruit juice, green tea, skim or soy milk instead.

5.) Replace half of the white flour in your baking recipes with whole-wheat flour, and only, use half the sweetener.

Taking Charge of Your Carb Intake

Here, you will learn how to manage your weight loss plan, which enables you to decrease your blood sugar and triglycerides level, assuming they're at a high.

You can have 5 carbohydrate (CHO) choices per day. One CHO choice doesn't go over the 15g of Total CHO per serving. A choice of CHO contains:

- o   1 slice of bread
- o   2 slices of slice bread at 40 calories
- o   1 small banana
- o   8-12 oz. beer, 3-4 oz. wine, or 1 oz. hard liquor

o Half a cup of spaghetti, macaroni, rice, oatmeal, or non-sugary cereal

o Half a cup of corn, potatoes, lima beans, pinto beans, green peas or black-eyed peas

I recommend you to eat:

✓ 6 servings of monounsaturated (you can find food like brewed coffee, vegetable oil and nuts rich in it) or polyunsaturated fat (in olive oil, nuts, cream cheese)

✓ 2 cups of 1/2% or 1% milk daily (you can substitute sugar-free, fat-free instant pudding mixed with very low fat milk, sugar-free ice cream, low-fat sugar-free yogurt, or sugar-free frozen yogurt)

Don't forget these guidelines:

o Check your weight (once a week would be appropriate)

o Drink 8-oz glass of water 8 times per day

o Eat whole grains

o Don't skip a meal (eat three to four meals a day) Eat only "green light" food if you eat between your meals

o Always read food labels carefully

o Start exercising and maintain it

- Make it a goal to be satisfied with eating non-fat or low-fat dairy, raw, lightly cooked, or "green light" (protein, fresh fruits and veggies, nuts/ seeds, super healthy oils like olives, coconut and flax) and food quality versus aiming for a certain level of calories
- Eat lean cuts of protein meat
- Monitor your whole foods weight loss diet progress. Track how often you eat chips, fast food, dessert or soda
- Be strict in following the Whole Foods diet plan 90% of the time
- You can treat yourself to a food craving 10% of the time
- Be patient, realistic and do not expect a "quick fix"
- Consult your doctor regarding your cholesterol level, blood sugar level, energy and blood pressure.

Nutritional Recommendations for the Whole Foods Diet

In order to maintain a healthy, smooth-going diet working with the whole foods, I've provided a food table you need to keep in mind. The first three columns are food you can have, and food high in fat and sugar and drink should be very, very limited. Just be consistent with following the list and later on in transition, you'll be happy you did.

Fruits and vegetables

Fresh

Frozen

Canned

Dried

100% fruit or vegetable drink Pure fruit juice smoothie (a portion a day)

Milk and dairy

Milk (or calcium fortified soya)

Cheese

Yogurt

Fromage frais

Non-dairy protein

Meat (bacon, sausages, beef, etc.)

Fish (tuna, sardines, fish fingers, etc.)

Poultry

Eggs

Beans

Starchy carbohydrates

Bread

(replace with whole wheat)

Pasta

(replace with whole wheat)

Potatoes (low fat oven chips)

Pasta

(replace with whole wheat)

Yams

Breakfast cereal

(replace with whole wheat)

White rice (brown rice instead)

Cornmeal

Millet

Maize

Oats

Food high in sugar or fat

Butter

Margarine

Low fat spread

Oil-based salad dressing

Cooking oil

Cream

Mayonnaise

Fried food

Crisps

Chocolate

Biscuits

Pastries

Pudding

Ice cream

Rich sauces

Gravy

Food and drinks in sugar

Soda (not diet)

Jam

Sweets

Puddings

Biscuits

Cakes

Pastries

Ice cream

some of the food and drink you can eat, drink or not eat and not drink during your diet, you should know how much of it to you're allowed to consume in order to get a the proper balance of nutrients.

1.) Fruits and vegetables

As much as you can, chow down on this! You have all the freedom to choose from a broad variation, so you can select your fruits and veggies with at least 5 different portions per day.

(One portion = 80g)

For example, you can choose between:

1 bowl of salad

A medium-sized apple

3 heaping tablespoons of peas

Fruit juice serving

Vegetable juice

Smoothie

2.) Milk and dairy

For the milk and dairy category, you're required only to eat moderately. With only 3 servings of calcium a day, your body has what it needs fully. Always pick the low fat kind as much as you can, from reduced fat cheeses to low fat milk.

A serving of milk = 200ml glass

A serving of yogurt = 150g of a small pot

A serving of cheese = 30g

3.) Non-dairy protein

You should also just consume moderate amounts of non-dairy protein. Beans and pulses such as soya, chickpeas, lentils or haricot can be eaten at 5 different portions a day. And like dairy, try to choose the low-in-fat versions as much as you're able to, cut out the fats in the meat, and skin poultry.

Fish are high in omega-3 fatty acids which help prevent the risk of heart attack. Two portions of fish per week are recommended, and one those portions should be saved for an oily fish such as mackerel, salmon or trout.

4.) Starchy carbohydrates

This is something you shouldn't miss out on in your diet. Sweet potato, yams and plantains... choose at least one food in every meal with a 1/3 base off this group on the food you eat daily.

For example:

Porridge oats (breakfast)

Potatoes with fish and veggies

Chicken salad sandwich

Stir-fried vegetables with rice

5.) Food high in sugar or fat/ food and drinks in sugar

Limit on this food group! Fat is still a significant constituent in health, because they contain high energy, but only up to very small amounts. If you insist on having it, at least pick out from the low or reduced fat section that have only 3 g per every 100.

Fats are split into three divisions. You have saturates, monounsaturates and the polyunsaturates.

Saturates

Remember to minimize your saturate consumption (biscuits, pastries, animal products, etc.) as these fats risk you higher of heart disease.

Tips to cut down on the saturates:

1.) Always refer to the nutrition facts on packaged goods.

2.) Remove fat and skin from meat and poultry.

3.) Buy lower fat meat and reduced fat dairy.

4.) Use fats minimally whenever fats are needed in cooking.

Monounsaturates and Polyunsaturates

In monosaturates and polyunsaturates, you can choose larger portions of fats and oils. (olive oil and sunflower oil) instead of butter, palm oil or lard from saturates.

Omegas 3 and 6 fatty acids

Omega-3 fatty acids found in food such as walnuts, soya oil and oily fish, as well as omega-6 fatty acids from vegetable oils (corn, sunflower, soya, etc.) should be part of the diet in small portions as these are very healthful.

Things you need to remember:

o Even though salt helps the body function, eat only 1/3 out of 6 g in a day as recommended for adults, and even less for children. Sodium is just 2.5 less of salt.

o While sugar sweetens your food, cut down on it as much as you can. It causes tooth decay.

o Drink 1.5 to 2 liters of fluids (water, fruit juice, tea, etc.) per day. Fluid intake varies depending on the individual's diet, age, physical activity and the weather

o Alcohol is permitted, but try to keep it at a low of about 3-4 units (for men) and 2-3 units (for women) per day. One unit = 25ml of spirits, so maybe you can take in a small glass of wine which is around 100 ml or 1/2 pint of standard strength beer, cider or lager on a daily basis.

o Women who are pregnant must maintain a balance diet of healthy food.

o Remember that supplements aren't alternatives to a healthy diet. Keep away from those kind that especially contain only single vitamins with high doses (may be unnecessary and medical advice is needed). A multivitamin or two is beneficial once in a while if you aren't meeting the nutrient requirements.

The Plant-Based Whole Foods Diet

Aside from the statistic that choosing plant-based protein over animal-based is less costly, protein from plants provides many benefits on health. They are mainly high in fiber and contain plenty of vitamins plus a variation of nutrition other than protein. They are found to have less calories and fat.

The fact that humans require 10% of calories derived of protein makes whole plant food ideal because they have exactly this much. Early studies have shown that too much protein based off animals eventually leads to a lesser life span. For two decades, an American and Italian researcher tracked a thousand men and women in their middle ages, and learned that those who had a diet based mostly on animal protein, were stricken with cancer 4x as much, or were more likely to die of diabetes compared to people with low-protein diets.

This urged researchers to advise that Americans lower their day-to-day animal protein intake, especially at the age of 65 and up, where results showed with believability based in genuine health, educational and ethnic background that more protein consumption led to damaging factors as you grow older. If at least 20% of calories are derived from protein, it is a high-protein diet. Less than 10% from calories means protein is low.

While many people have relied heavily on the animal-based protein diet to lose weight faster, Valter Longo, a gerontology professor at the University of Southern California says that while it is successful, it is for a short-term only. A 2-month experiment was also done among mice, and it was discovered that those who had a significantly lower protein intake had a smaller size in tumor. In another find, Molochio, a small town in Italy, researchers discovered centenarians based their diet purely from plants, which in turn, allowed them to live at least 10 decades. We should instead be eating seeds, nuts or legumes, not pork, beef and lamb.

It is recommended by top health agencies to take in 0.8 g of protein for every kilogram of body weight every day. So let's say you weigh 150 lbs., you should be eating 8 or 9 ounces of meat, plus a few cups of dry beans. The risks of health become higher as you grow old.

A low-protein diet helps with healthy weight maintenance and safeguards them from feebleness.

Maybe you can start off with 1.5 grams of protein for each kilo of your body's weight. If you take in a variation of whole plant food and you are an active individual, your protein needs are met faster, allowing you to receive a good amount of protein for maintenance, growth and a fast metabolism. Consuming a good amount of whole plant foods heighten overall muscle size and performance, especially if you're athletic who requires ample amounts of protein.

Protein: Plant vs. Animal

Why don't you take the healthy alternative and get all the nutrition you need off plants rather than animals? Eating too much animal protein (over 10%) is proven to hold high repercussions on your health. Protein is high in acid. It leaks alkaline minerals in your body like the calcium from your bones.

Meat is also very toxic. It contains many antibiotics as well as artificial hormones from enhancer fodder given to animals. These toxins overwork your liver. They have to work extra hard just to get rid of these dangerous substances inside your body. Energy is used up 5x as much only for its digestion, which takes away the essential life force our bodies regularly require. Moreover, eating a lot of meat triggers an insulin response which leads to insulin and pancreatic deterioration, and sets off for type 2 diabetes.

In a study conducted in China, Dr. Campbell explains the direct connection between animal protein and cancer. Despite how 'lean' the meat in markets say they are, it doesn't escape the fact that they are loaded with fat and cholesterol, and we know that stroke, atherosclerosis and heart disease can fast come in this scenario. Choosing to go with a plant-based diet can help society as a whole. We aren't merely saving animals, we save ourselves and Mother Earth. But I won't go plunging into a battle of animal vs. plant protein, rather, I will provide you with accurate directions towards a safer, healthier lifestyle, a lifestyle that will also make you lose weight!

Below are more reasons why you should pick plant-based foods of animals:

Low in Fat

Animal-based protein shows a much higher fat concentration compared to plant protein. They are spiked with saturated and trans fats, which can cause heart disease. In comparison, you will find that a hundred grams of ground beef contains 21 g of fat, 24 g of protein, and only 0 g of fiber, while a hundred g of kidney beans have 23 grams of protein, 1 g of fat and 15 g of fiber.

High in Fiber

Aside from a decreasing risk of heart disease (plant has no cholesterol), did you know that fiber can only be found only in kidney beans, pulses, lentils, etc. and only plant food in general? They offer protein, but also with the extra benefits fiber can provide. Fiber leaves your stomach feeling satisfied for a longer period, and prevents food compulsions, which allows you to manage your appetite altogether. Fiber also improves your digestive health by promoting regular bowels.

The doubt on whether or not you can get enough protein in a plant-based diet can be answered confidently: Don't worry! You'll never get sick because of too much protein, and you will always get the protein your body needs. Did you know that our body actually requires less protein than you thought it should get on a daily basis? World Health Organization says that a male weighing 150 lbs, in his 2,000 calorie diet, only needs 22.5 of daily protein, which is 4.5 % of calories from protein. A pregnant woman must get 6%. The Food and Nutrition Board recommends 6% for individuals, while other health organizations say you can go by at least 2.5%. But majority of Americans eat above 20% , so that won't be a problem. Tell me, have you ever seen someone or heard of someone sick because of protein deficiency? Even the strongest and biggest animals of the forest, the gorillas, the elephants, the hippos, they all eat plants!

There is a wide range of plant-based food rich in protein such as:

Spinach: 51%

Beans: 26%

Corn: 12%

Mushrooms: 35%

Potatoes: 11%

Oatmeal 16%

Whole wheat pasta 15%

Maybe you can try to survey some plant-based food at the supermarket on your next trip.

Plants High in Protein

A lot of people who are conscious about their health, like vegetarians, have a story to share on how they became successful with transitioning to a healthy eating lifestyle. No matter their story, the challenge for non-meat eaters, is how to get enough protein in their diet plan.

One of the significant components our bodies need for it to function properly is protein. However, too much of it leads to many types of disease. But think how our ancestors, who were hunters, had to live with back in the primitive age. They only ate 20% of meat in their daily diet, and still managed to become strong, expert survivalists. So it isn't exactly going to be the toughest stage to live through contrary to what others may believe. You just have to learn how to go above the temptation of fast food and other easy-to-nuke products this second millennium has to offer.

Protein can be harmful because unlike fats and carbs, our bodies cannot store it. An excess of protein will leave our liver and kidneys strained. Its surplus acts as acid inside our bodies. Despite what they say, you can live on greens alone without the calorie-clad food like eggs, meat or dairy. Even if you are living a highly active lifestyle, as long as your diet is a well-rounded selection of plant-based whole food, you can still get more than enough protein.

It's safer to take on a diet that offers variety rather than rely on one nutrient. Consider how eating protein that comes from plants can provide you with fiber and nutrition. If you are instead in a diet that consists primarily of plant-based food, you will get neither too much nor too little protein, but just the amount your body needs. Below, I'll give you a list that tops the category for high protein content plant-based food.

Legumes – The base work of many diets for centuries

1 cup lentils (18 g)

1 cup refried beans (15.5 g)

1 oz peanuts – (6.5 g)

1 cup soybeans (28 g)

1 cup tempeh – (great as veggie burger, alternative to meatballs) (30 g)

1 cup pinto, kidney, black beans (13-15 g)

1 cup garbanzo beans and hummus (14.5 g)

Nuts and seeds - a staple for most vegan and vegetarian dieters

1/4 cup (2 oz.) walnuts (5 g)

1 oz. cashews (4.4 g)

1 oz. pistachios (5.8 g)

2 tbsp almonds (4 g)

1 oz. sesame seeds 6.5 grams, 3 tbsp of tahini (8 g)

Nut butters (almond, peanut and cashew butter - 2 tbsp has about 8 g of protein)

Vegetables - the backbone of all diets

1 cup broccoli (5 g)

1 avocado (10 g)

1 cup spinach (5 g)

1 cup boiled peas (9 g)

1 cup cooked sweet potato (5 g)

2 cups cooked kale – (5 g)

Non-dairy milk

Almond, ancient grain, soy - 1 cup = 7-9 g of protein

Supplements

Hemp (high in omega-6 and omega-3) (30 g of hemp powder in a smoothie, cereal, salad, rice, etc. = 11 g of protein)

Spirulina and chlorella (used by vegans and vegetarians). They are rich in protein and

nutrients, has all the amino acids.

Grains

Amaranth, bulgur, brown rice, oat bran, wheat germ, etc. (grains high in protein)

Oatmeal - 1 cup (6 g)

Quinoa (rice or pasta alternative, can be breakfast cereal (w/ almond milks and berries),

and good served with vegetables) - 1 cup (9 g)

Sprouted, ancient, multi-grains – a big portion of the diet

Sprouted grain bread products (bread, buns, tortillas).You can get 7-10 g of bread in a

wrap or sandwich.

Wheat gluten

Seitan (24 g). This is a good supplement to fish, beef and soy products

Tips on how to start:

Try keeping a journal to record your current diet. This includes every portion of food and beverage in all your meals, not leaving out the condiments such as butter. Once you have this, you will be more aware about what you're eating and realize you have to start change fast. Be mindful not to miss out on anything you eat or drink within the day.

You will then have to slowly start replacing the food you eat on a regular basis with plant-based ones. Try consuming lesser calories by swapping a bag of potato chips with apples as a snack, or a plate of vegetables vs. a large steak with mashed potatoes topped with gravy. This doesn't mean that you can never enjoy a plate of steak ever again, moderation is just an important factor to train yourself with once you start your diet. It starts with small changes. You can go meatless on one of the weekends, cut down on processed fats like cheese or yogurt (have coconut or non-dairy yogurt with soy instead), enjoy a fruit smoothie vs. a bottle of soda, have oatmeal with rice milk vs. a sugary cereal or slowly let go of meat products (substitute with seitan or tempeh). Sooner or later you can treat yourself by eating meat but removing the oils and butter.

Remember that on those days where you want to eat animal-based food, always follow the rule of 80/10/10. This means that 80% of you plate must include raw or cooked vegetables, while 10% must have whole grains (quinoa, amaranth or brown rice), and the remaining 10%, the animal protein you choose for that day. This enables you to eat a wider selection of plant-based food as you gradually transition your lifestyle and diet.

These tiny but smart steps will empower you and teach you to start eating maybe 2-3 plant-based meals a week, and on to 2 out of 3 vegetarian meals in a day. It's also not a bad move to try a variety of uncommon-to-America exotic dishes from around the world. Whether it's Moroccan, Latin American or Southeast Asian with an infusion of healthy spice, this is a good way to orient yourself with dishes that typify healthy eating.

Healthy food starts with whole foods. And do not worry about your budget plan, I have an ample of budgeting tips you can take as you read onward. You will find that the plant-based whole foods budget will not only provide you the basic nutrients that your body needs, but that the natural process develops into losing weight faster.

If you've always wanted to shed off those pounds the natural way, the healthy way, this is the best diet plan I can share to you. So not only do you save, you become healthy. Believe in it with me today!

Transitioning to the Whole Foods Diet

Taking a leap to a new diet you're still slightly unfamiliar with may seem daunting. You doubt if you can forego with following every rule or master self-control. Don't worry, it's normal to be concerned by things like these. As long as you keep your focus in mind, your goal to lose weight and to eat healthy, then you're getting a step closer to your destination.

Baby Step 1: Learning to let go

Take a good look into your refrigerator and cupboards, locate all the processed food (e.g. canned soup, junk food, pudding, salad dressing, frozen pizza, etc.), remove them one by one, and drop them in the trash bag. Progressively, you'll ease into replacing them with healthy choices like palm sugar, organic butter, whole grain flour, honey, fresh veg and more.

This may be hard to do at first, but trust me, the pain will pass. Rather than thinking what a waste, think of the actual waste that gets inside your body when you keep eating bad food. Get rid of the sugary, the painstakingly-processed as fast as you can now. If you ever get sidetracked with the good food you're used to, there is a wide array of resources in my book, so don't hesitate to find a counterpart that's just as, or maybe even more filling.

Try these tips:

Pack your lunch for work. It guarantees you don't have to buy fast food and other junk, you'll get a whole wheat preparation instead. Less expensive too, if we're looking at the bigger picture.

Read and review. Please try to avoid buying food from the supermarket that contains more than 5 ingredients, because they're likely to be loaded with unnatural fixings. Also, take the time to know the ingredients you buy.

Baby Step 2: Keeping things basic

Picture your grocery list simplified without the super long and pointless list with all kinds of convenience food. While starting from scratch with planning and cooking on a whole new list of ingredients may take some time to get used to, the whole foods diet list is pretty simple. Just keep in mind the categories:

o   Grains, beans, seeds and nuts

o   Fruits & veggies

o   Eggs & dairy

o   Meats (which include seafood and sometimes organ meat)

o   Sweeteners

o   Fats

o   Fermented food (homemade probiotics)

Baby Step 3: Food substituting like an expert

Looking for real food recipes may be an exciting endeavor, but also consider sticking to the option on what you know you can turn into a magically delicious and healthy meal. Although many Americans don't like to eat vegetables, substitutes (you'll get to know more about them later in the book) like tofu, tempeh, beans and seitan will get you hooked once you move forward. Change can happen over time, slowly, but certainly. Later in the book, you can take some of the recipes I've compiled.

Always remember to keep in mind and choose:

Organic milk over store brand milk

Keep away from drinking processed chemicals packed inside store brand milk. It's bursting with antibiotics and growth hormones fed to cows. Go whole, go healthy instead.

Carrots and hummus over potato chips

This is period is hard to overcome especially if you're used to a bag of potatoes for your mid-afternoon. Chips are dangerous, just remember. They're packed with corn syrup solids and partially hydrogenated soybean oil. Even the baked ones are a lie. Try veggies with hummus dip instead. There are a variety flavors like artichoke. It may be bland at first but you will learn to appreciate it, and trust me, you'll get the hang of it. Hey, it's for your own good.

Homemade smoothie over yogurt smoothie

Yogurt bought in the store may not be as healthy as it claims itself to be. Syrup, sugar and artificial flavors hide behind riboflavin and B vitamins and you miss out on the whole-food nutrients. Going homemade is healthier and less costly. Use fresh fruit and veggies and be creative with your yogurt at home

Homemade tabouleh over creamy dip

Ranch, creamy dill, French onion…these go so well with chips. But they're both processed food chockfull of fat and sodium. Try making an avocado dip or tabouleh yourself. You just have to soak bulgur wheat in warm water for 15 minutes, add some cucumber, garlic powder, parsley, tomatoes, dill spice, and mint, and use this as dip for tortilla chips or veggies instead of potato chips. Tabouleh is tasty and healthy!

And some more to look out for:

o Honey with a bit of molasses over brown sugar
o Brown rice syrup over corn syrup
o Whole wheat pastry flour/ white whole wheat flour over white flour (A/P flour)
o Maple syrup or honey over white sugar
o Baking soda over baking powder
o Non-fat, plain Greek yogurt over sour cream
o Heart healthy oils (e.g. olive, avocado oil or organic butter from pastured or grass-fed cows) over butter

Baby Step 4: Set out on one homemade probiotic and keep it consistent

Because of today's mass-produced anti-bacterial products, anti-biotics and genetically modified food, homemade probiotics are more crucial than ever before. They are potent immune-boosters. They sheathe our bodies with good bacteria. So go homemade. Try searching for Kvass, sauerkraut, water kefr recipes, fermented condiments online. You will find dozens to help you.

Baby Steps 5: Outwit sweet, fattening temptations

Driven as you are to keep away from packaged food and sticking to purely homemade goods like homemade cake with homemade icing with edible designs, please refrain from thinking that you must reinvent every snack known to man. Cut out on eggs and dairy. Even if your family, especially the kids relish on these, be trained to halt the impulse. Learning how to become truly satisfied with just the good and healthy stuff will catch on quick, and snacking will soon be a bygone.

Baby Steps Tip 6: Don't think all packaged goods are a complete beware

Yes, I know I've mentioned earlier that packaged food is loaded with additives, artificial colorings, GMOs and more, but it doesn't mean EVERY packaged good is a total restriction. We can entertain a few exceptions on the plate because not every food we make homemade can be made from scratch.

Here are a few staple to include in your whole foods diet:

- Canned wild-caught salmon & tuna (BPA-free)
- Canned organic tomato sauce and paste (BPA-free)
- Grass-fed hot dogs (just occasionally because they are quite pricey)
- Jarred artichoke hearts
- Jarred sundried tomatoes
- Jarred organic pasta sauce
- Organic jam
- Organic pie fillings (pumpkin puree, etc.)
- Organic condiments (mustard, mayo, BBQ sauce, etc.)
- Organic coconut milk (replaces condensed milk)
- Whole Foods for Asian dishes (chestnuts, canned water chestnuts, miso, etc.)
- Whole grain pasta (sprouted whole-grain pasta is even better)

It's all about making effort and overcoming the newness of transition. From getting rid of white flour to learning to bake without white sugar, in the end you'll be very pleased by the turnout of your diet. Even if you had an exhausting day and feel like rewarding yourself with a sumptuous slice of pizza, that's fine, you can reboot again tomorrow. Reflect on it the next day and be more prepared to control the situation the next time something like this happens. Just remember, baby steps.

Whole Foods Cooking on a Budget

While some individuals currently on a diet plan have all the means of maintenance and even manage to purchase pricier ingredients, this book is made especially for those who are on a tight budget. I created this book to serve as an easy guide if you're seeking for better, less costly alternatives that still work. Here, you will learn the best places to buy whole foods, what should be in your whole foods shopping cart, whole foods cooking tips and much more. It's good to be anticipative!

Whole Foods Shopping Cart

Shopping for whole foods as a beginner may prove a bit more challenging. For this reason, I have compiled a list of whole food items that you can easily find in your local grocery store. Simply mix these ingredients up by following my example recipes found in the latter part of the book and you've got yourself a promising diet.

What to Buy:

Whole Grains:

Amaranth	100% Whole wheat flour
Barley	100% Whole-wheat or whole-grain bread
Brown rice	100% Whole-wheat pasta or couscous
Buckwheat – hot cereal or flour	100% Whole-wheat pitas or tortillas
Bulgur (cracked wheat)	Whole-grain breakfast cereal (Millet or Buckwheat)
Flaxseed	Oats
Spelt	Steel cut oatmeal
Wheat Berries	Wild rice

Fresh or frozen vegetables (organic is preferable)

Artichoke	Green beans
Asparagus	Kale
Baby spinach	Leek
Beets	Mushroom
Broccoli	Onions
Bell pepper	Parsnip
Carrot	Radish
Cauliflower	Rutabaga
Chard	Shallot
Celery	Squash
Collard	Sweet potato
Cucumber	Tomato
Garlic	Turnip

Spices, sweeteners and condiments

Balsamic vinegar	Unsweetened cocoa powder
Naturally sweetened ketchup	Mustard with no added sugar
Pure herbs and spices	Non-fat Greek yogurt
Grape seed oil	Walnut oil
Safflower oil	Extra virgin olive oil

Local organic honey   Stevia

Organic maple syrup

Canned or Jarred items

Light Coconut Milk   Olives

                                Low   sodium,   no   sugar
Sun-dried tomatoes   marinara

                                Vegetable   or   chicken
                                stock/broth - no sugar or
                                dextrose added, and very little
Water-soaked tuna in can   or no sodium

Unsweetened fruit   Pumpkin in can (not filling)

Canned beans - no sugar and
as much as possible very little
or no added sodium   Tuna packed in water

Tomato paste or sauce with
very little or no sodium   Unsweetened fruit

Tip: Acidic products such as pineapple are better bought in glass
jars.

Dried Fruits and Nuts

Raisins

Almonds

Walnuts

Dried cranberries

Pistachios

Sweetened fruit juice

Dried apricots (no sugar)

Lean meats (organic is preferable)

All kinds of fish (canned tuna is recommended)

Boneless and skinless chicken breast

Bison

Eggs

Ground beef (extra lean)

Ground turkey (extra lean)

Venison

Cherries

Dry or canned beans and legumes

Adzuki beans

Black beans

Chickpeas

Kidney beans

Lentils

Navy beans

Pinto beans

Dairy (organic is preferable)

Whole milk (for kids)

String cheese/ shredded cheese

Organic low fat cottage cheese

Stonyfield Oikos Vanilla/ Chobani/ Plain Greek yogurt

Unsweetened Vanilla Almond Milk

Egg whites in carton

Free range eggs

Drinks

Chai or green tea bags

Honest Tea

Kombucha

Organic coffee

Chai or green tea bags

Honest Tea

Kombucha

Packaged products

Coconut oil spray

Chia seeds

Flaxseed meal

Hummus

Larabar

Naturally sweetened whey protein

Old Fashioned Oats/ Steel- Cut Oats

Fresh/ frozen, sugarless or fruits (organic is preferable)

Apples   Nectarines

Apricots Oranges

Berries   Pears

Bananas Peaches

Blackberries Pineapple

Blueberries   Plums

Cantaloupe   Plutos

Cherries Pomegranates

Grapefruits   Raspberries

Grapes   Star fruit

Kiwi   Strawberries

Lemons Watermelon

Nuts/Nut Butters

Almond butter (ingredients should contain only almonds and some salt)

All-natural peanut butter

Raw almonds

Raw sunflower seeds

Bread

Ezekiel bread (plain and cinnamon raisin)

Ezekiel English muffins

Whole grain tortillas

Whole Grain Pita Pockets

Whole Grain Waffles

Whole Foods Diet Staples

There are a few essential staple food you need to equip yourself with as you set out toward the whole foods diet. I have categorized them into three so you can easily purchase them and pick them out of their designated storage places.

Frozen Must-Haves
- o Whole-grain flours and whole-wheat breadcrumbs
- o Pre-made stored dishes (soup, ravioli, sauce, etc.)
- o Pre-made baked goods
- o Home-made soup (vegetable broth, chili or tomato sauce)
- o Home-made muffins, granola bars, waffles
- o Extra whole-grain breads and tortilla
- o Locally raised meat and seafood
- o Organic vegetables like peas and corn
- o Frozen fruits (e.g. organic berries [for berry sauce or smoothies])

Pantry Must-Haves
- o Fresh fruits (apples, avocados, lemons, etc.)
- o Nuts and seeds (raw almonds, cashews, chia, hemp, sunflower, etc.)

- Organic applesauce (in case you run out of fresh fruit)
- Baking ingredients (baking soda and powder, vanilla extract, salt, unrefined sugar, coconut flakes, raw honey, cocoa powder, dark chocolate, etc.)
- Packaged products (raisins, canned tuna, coconut milk, canned beans, palm oil, coconut oil, balsamic vinegar, apple cider vinegar, pure maple syrup, etc.)
- Whole-grain products (whole-grain bread, whole-grain cereal, quinoa, millet, brown rice, etc.)
- Dried goods (dried fruit, dried beans, rolled oats, oat flour, oat flour, spelt flour, raw almonds, potato, herbs and spices, onions, garlic, etc.)

Refrigerated Must-Haves
- Eggs
- Soy sauce
- Ghee
- Lard
- Perishable fruits and veggies
- Unsalted organic butter
- Healthy snacks (e.g. olives)
- "All-fruit" jelly and 1-ingredient peanut butter
- Spread and sauces (salad dressing, mustard, maple syrup, etc.)

- o Dairy products (almond milk, yogurt, etc.)
- o Organic and non GMO tofu or tempeh (for rare occasions)
- o Fresh veggies (carrots, kale, spinach, celery, broccoli, etc.)

Try stocking up an entire whole foods list for only $99!

1.8 kilos of dried beans (black, pinto, white, lentils)

1 2-oz pkg arame sea vegetable
1 16-oz jar tahini (ground sesame seed butter)
1 10-oz bottle reduced-sodium tamari soy sauce

1 32-oz bottle organic apple cider vinegar
1 6-oz bottle Bragg Liquid Aminos

1 32-oz box low-sodium organic vegetable broth
1 32-oz box organic unsweetened soymilk
1 32-oz box organic unsweetened almond milk
1 14-oz can organic lite coconut milk

1 6-oz can tomato paste
1 18-oz jar organic no-salt-added peanut or almond butter
1 8-oz pkg organic mellow white miso

1 8-oz squeeze bottle organic Dijon mustard

2 14.5-oz cans no-salt-added diced tomatoes

4 15-oz cans no-salt-added beans (black, garbanzo, kidney, pinto)

7 oz each organic unsulfured apricots, dates and raisins
8 oz each organic raw almonds, walnuts and sunflower seeds
4 lbs whole grains (1 quinoa, 1 pearled barley, 2 long-grain brown rice)
2 lbs whole-wheat pasta of your choice
2 lbs rolled / steel-cut oats

Health Food at $2

Cut down on food cost by making homemade meals that exhibit the finest healthy goods from the supermarket. Instead of white rice, cookies or frozen pizza, buy whole grains, vegetables or beans. Fortunately many of these whole foods cost less than $2. For example, a lb. of brown rice is just $1.75 and cooks up to 10 side servings!

Read the list I compiled below. You'll get some tips on $2 food you can easily buy. (Cost varies depending on store, area and time of the year).

1. 100% Whole-Wheat Bread

What's in one serving? 2 slices. 1 slice of bread = 28 g

Nutrients per serving (2 slices): Roughly 120 calories, 6 g protein, and 3 g fiber.

Good for: Sandwiches, bread pudding, bread stuffing and breakfast strata.

What's it going to cost? A 22-ounce store-brand loaf of whole-wheat bread is $1.99 on sale. One loaf has around 22 slices, making 11 servings at 2 slices per serving. That makes it 18 cents per serving.

2. Whole-Wheat or Multigrain Pasta

What's in one serving? 2 ounces of dried pasta. A serving for most people is equal to about 2 ounces of dried pasta. You can get around 7 servings in a standard box.

Nutrients per serving: Roughly 200 calories, 7 g protein, and 6 g fiber.

Good for: Pasta dishes

What's it going to cost? A store-brand 13- to 16 ounce box/ bag is about $1.69. So that's approximately 24 cents.

3. Brown Rice

What's in one serving? 1/4 cup dry rice.

Nutrients per serving: 170 calories, 2 g fiber, and 4 g protein.

Good for: Side dishes, fried rice, casseroles, rice salads, stews, and soups.

What's it going to cost? A 1 lb. bag = $1.75 that makes 10 servings. So it's around 18 cents per serving.

4. Frozen Vegetables

What's in one serving? 1 cup

Nutrients per serving: A classic mix cup, serving of frozen mixed vegetables has 82 calories, 6 g fiber, 4 g protein, 7% of the Daily Value for potassium, 115% of the vitamin A Daily Value, and 8% of the Daily Value.

Good for: Side dishes, casseroles, and stews.

What's it going to cost? Approximately 25 cents. Frozen vegetables come in 12-ounce to 24-ounce bags that cost anywhere from $1.75 to $2.25. They contain 6-8 cups. You can purchase a bag frozen organic green beans for only $1.79 at a national store. A bag of petite peas is $1.19, and a 10-ounce box of frozen chopped spinach is $1.19.

5. Canned Refried Beans

What's in one serving? One serving can make around 3.5 servings based on 1/2-cup servings.

Nutrients per serving: Around 140 calories (vegetarian beans), 7 g protein, 6 g fiber, 4% of the calcium Daily Value, and 10% of the iron Daily Value.

Good for: Burritos, enchiladas, nachos, dips, side dish.

What's it going to cost? You can buy a 15-ounce can of store brand vegetarian refried beans for around $1.19, making it cost about 34 cents per serving.

6. Nonfat Greek Yogurt

What's in one serving? Most individual servings come in 6-ounce or 8-ounce containers. Save money and buy a bigger container of Greek yogurt. Take out the 6- or 8-ounce portion from it.

Nutrients per serving: 150 calories, 0 g fiber, and 14 g protein (for a 6-ounce serving of honey vanilla)

Good for: A quick snack, smoothies, or parfaits made with granola and fruit.

What's it going to cost? About 89 cents per individual serving. 6- to 8-ounce containers cost around 89 cents or less when on sale.

Where to Buy Whole Foods, Tips and Experiences

If you're looking for fresh, nutritious food reinvented along with great taste and appearance, I recommend you drop by the Whole Foods Market. This is my favorite whole foods go-to food shop.

Did you know that Whole Foods Market, Inc. is now the leading global retailer for organic and natural food? With stores in the USA, Canada, UK and now Australia, revenue peaked at $19.757 billion this 2014 since opening its first location on September 20, 1980 in Austin, Texas. This is the perfect t place to drop by as you kick off your exciting new diet plan. They sell the highest quality food at competitive prices.

You can also drop by these competitor markets that sell healthy food:

Wild Oats Market

Established in Boulder, Colorado Wild Oats Market is well-known for its fine organic food.

Sprouts Farmers Market

Get the feel of the good old-fashion farmers market. With great value on local products, Sprouts offers the best of wholesome nuts, grains, fresh fruits and veggies. Try their full-service delis that sell all kinds of seafood and meat.

Fairway Market

From a stand that started out in Manhattan, Fairway continues to open 3-4 new stores all over the US yearly.

Trader Joe's

With 80% of its stock bearing their own brand name, Trader Joe's is known as the neighborhood grocery store. From vegetarian food, unusual frozen goods, to imported wine, you can find just about any food and even non-food product here.

H-E-B

With now over 350 stores throughout Texas including Northern Mexico, this outstanding supermarket ranked 13th in "Top 75 North American Food Retailers" in 2008.

Wegmans

Wegmans is popular for selling basic commodities at lower costs versus other nationwide brands. They're in Fortune's list of "100 Best Companies to Work For".

Budget-minded Tips for Wholesome Shopping

It's time to kick off your whole foods diet! Before beginning, keep in mind budget consideration is very important. I think many of you agree with me that just because we are now going the whole foods route, doesn't mean we shouldn't be mindful of expenditure. Just remember that if you buy things in a box or can, it's never good for you, and you're probably paying for too much.

Being in a whole foods budget diet is much easier than you think. If you are eager to pursue the whole foods diet on a regular basis, but are worried that it may be a bit pricier than your average grocery plan, I have some tips you can follow that will help make your whole foods diet successful without burdening your budget. To start, I will share to the the need-to-knows you have to take with you when going shopping for whole foods in the grocery store. One: always use cash, and second, pay attention to the list.

1.) **Using cash versus credit** is a wise move. *Predictably Irrational* author, Dan Ariely, posits that generally, people find it more of a bigger loss when paying with cash, and the least damaging when using credit! I agree this mindset must be discontinued. If you really put some thought to it, adding on to your electronic tab is more detrimental than life-saving. Here's what you should do: when you've finalized a budget plan, withdraw the exact amount from the atm right away and bring it with you to the grocery store. In this manner, you can't possibly stray from your budget, and will even aim for the lower priced purchases.

2.) **By sticking to the list**, you are eliminating all possible circumstances of having to add on to it. Getting rid of temptation is something you have to practice on a regular basis because grocery stores have a way of trying to pique your pocket whether it's displaying a discounted bag of sweets or a set of cosmetics before the pay counter.

3.) **Early bird shopping** allows you to do your shopping a lot faster, and refrains you from spending on unplanned snacks or meals. You don't need to be tempted to grab a bag of Cheetos on the way home. Go before lunch hour hits.

4.) **Buy ingredients locally.** Local farmer goods are freshly picked and organic. You can even speak to the farmer for some advice on healthy food!

5.) **Buy by bulk.** Whole wheat products such as barley, brown rice, cornmeal, as well as meat, becomes far cheaper when you them in bulk. The cost is just the same and even lower than the small size packages you see in the supermarket.

6.) **Buy meat frozen.** Yes, you can do this. Some butcher shops do not sell their meat offhand but place them in the freezer first. Chicken and turkey breast, and especially frozen fish will sell at a much lower price. Also, be sure to ask if they were taken from a safe source.

7.) **Pass up on packaged goods** as much as you can. Skipping the packaged food aisle will reward you plenty. Instead of buying a can of beans, for less its price, buy a pound of dried beans. They can actually make as much as 3 cans when you cook them. Also, stop buying boxes of flavored rice, you can get more pounds of basmati rice for the same price which can make you a month's worth of oatmeal. The cost is lesser than a box of individual oatmeal packets.

8.) Buy vegetables with stems and leaves. You'll be able to get the most out of your produce. You can use carrot tops for broth and its peelings for soup. Beet greens, kohlrabi leaves can be salad ingredients. Radish leaves and broccoli stems are edible too. Also, know how to prioritize when you shop organic. Buy organic thin-skinned fruits, as well as regular thick-skinned fruits.

9.) Buy produce in season. It's more economical, and you get more benefits health-wise! In-season produce is usually hand-picked before ripping. Try buying strawberries in April instead of a month later. Fresh is best.

10.) Include lesser priced protein on your meals. While many dieters might want to have free-range chicken breasts or grass-fed beef two times a day, the average price can be too hefty. Instead, top an adequate amount of wholesome protein with some farm fresh eggs, beans, organic milk, nuts or low-fat cheese.

11.) Choose a store to shop in regularly. After which, I recommend you create a plan to visit that store during your free period. Try purchasing from the internet (for example, Azure Standard, a bulk health food supplier over showy health food stores. Items like parmesan cheese and almond meal flour are so much cheaper).

12.) Save some money even for items not on sale. Make a list of what you're supposed to buy in every store so you can try out several products. A lot of produce on sale are also at the peak of freshness. You can buy extra and freeze them. You can freeze fruits and veggies like peppers, tomatoes and berries. Also, try to be more economic like minimizing the meat you use in some of your recipes. Do comparisons and survey better deals. Reuse leftover ingredients like bones to make soup broth.

13.) Use your free sunlit space at home. Do you have spare room for a pot of herbs or spices? How's the garage front, balcony and what about the corner on top of your kitchen sink below the window? It's a pleasant feeling to know you eat your veggies home-grown and fresh!

14.) Reward yourself one treat per week. You've done a good job abstaining. No reason to hinder yourself from food favorites for very long.

15.) Looking out for coupon or recipe flyers help you find the best ingredients around town on sale. If coupons mention the word "ANY" in the product description (e.g. "any canned beans), then you can you can take advantage of that coupon and use it for any other product manufactured by the same company.

You can sign up among the list of companies that have coupons for organic products:

o   Whole Foods Market
o   Common Kindness
o   Coupons.com
o   Earthbound Farms
o   Mambo Sprouts

- Ibotta Cash Back App
- Recycle Bank

16.) Organizing a meal plan every week before hitting the grocery store is important. Knowing what you will eat for the week, apart from that sense of well-prepared accomplishment, makes quite a big difference on the amount of food you might have to dump in the garbage due to spoiling. Planning out your menu after you shop is also good because it enables you to keep in line with your budget. You won't be shopping for special ingredients to create meals that are pre-planned. This also helps keep unintended budget purchases from going to the waste bin as you're carrying out the planned menu.

Whole Foods Meal Plan Samples

Are you excited to fix up a whole foods meal? To get you on your way and make things easier, I'm going to share to you some of the whole foods meals and ingredients that I have put together. For variation, I interchange my selections, so you're free to which meals for that week you'd want to repeat.

Here are a few good ingredients you can whip into a wholesome meal. First follow this list and buy the ff. ingredients:

Shopping List 1

- Bag of organic blue corn tortilla chips

- Salsa

- Dry red wine

- Mustard

- 4 Canned diced tomatoes

- 2 Cans tomato sauce

- 2 Cans of tomato paste

- 2 Cans of kidney beans

- 2 Cans refried beans

- Flour tortillas

- Celery

- Carrots, large bag

- 4 Zucchinis

- Blueberries, fresh or frozen

- Apples

- 1 lemon

- Spinach

- Breakfast sausage (any type)

- Orange juice

- Swiss cheese

- 2 Monterey Jack cheese

- Mozzarella cheese

- Parmesan cheese (shredded)

- 2 jars Marinated artichoke hearts

- Maple syrup

- Almonds

- Oats, old fashioned

- Box macaroni noodles

- Can of green chilies

- Can of black olives

- 2 lbs. Cheddar cheese

- Cottage cheese

- Cream cheese

- Sour cream

- Corn (or taco size flour) tortillas, depending on preference

- Chicken broth

- Mushrooms

- Lettuce

- 2-4 Avocadoes

- Green onions

- 2 Green bell peppers

- Red bell pepper

- Onions

- Potatoes, baking

- Bag of new potatoes

- Frozen shrimp

- Frozen halibut or other whitefish

86

- 2 bags Frozen broccoli

- Frozen California mix (cauli/broccoli/carrots)

- Frozen corn

- Frozen green beans

- Frozen peas

- Milk

- Eggs

- Thin sliced turkey breast

- 2 lbs. Ground turkey or beef

- 4 lbs. Beef roast

- Whole wheat bread

- Corn bread mix

Then you can use these to make mean meals at breakfast, lunch and dinner, all throughout!

Breakfast:

- Mini Muffin Quiches, fresh fruit (freeze extra green onions for future use)

- Mexican breakfast casserole (this can make a big 9x13 casserole dish, good for 2 days for 4-6 people)

- Honey orange French toast

- Baked oatmeal

- Oven-baked oatmeal, served with blueberries, maple syrup and butter (make a double batch for use two days in the week)

Lunch:

- Apple turkey cheese quesadillas

- Homemade macaroni and cheese with vegetable crudites

- Zucchini vegetable soup served with bread

- Spinach artichoke dip served with organic corn tortilla chips or fresh fruit and toasted bread

- Nachos. Place corn tortilla chips in a large casserole dish. Top with refried beans, cooked, and cheese. Warm casserole in oven at 350F until the cheese melts. Serve with salsa, avocados and sour cream

Dinner:

- Broccoli Cheese Soup served with bread and butter

- Chili (use turkey or ground beef)) and cornbread

- Vegetable Beef Soup. Dice beef to fine pieces. Add additional broth or water along with 1 can of diced tomatoes or leftover vegetables you may have (corn, potatoes, green beans, zucchini, are good).

- Shrimp Quesadillas. Serve with Mexican sty le rice, beans and sour cream.

- Honey Mustard Halibut. Serve with baked potatoes and buttered California mix (broccoli/cauliflower/carrots).

- Tacos. Serve with all the trimmings: ground beef, refried beans, diced black olives, avocados, , shredded lettuce and cheese and salsa)

- Slow cooker beef, vegetables, bread and butter

Shopping List 2

- canned black eyed peas
- can black olives
- can stewed tomatoes
- 2 cans tomato saucc
- salsa
- 2 cans green chiles
- Swiss cheese, sliced
- Cheddar cheese, 3 blocks
- Monterey Jack cheese
- canned tuna
- loaf of bread
- croissants
- frozen green beans
- frozen corn
- frozen peas
- frozen salmon fillets
- head cauliflower

- 1 lemon
- bag spinach
- 4 avocadoes
- 6 tomatoes
- premade pizza crust
- sour cream, 2 cartons
- cream cheese
- carton cottage cheese
- bag of new potatoes
- milk
- pint half and half
- bacon
- eggs
- large carton plain y yogurt
- flour tortillas
- frozen shrimp
- chicken breasts
- 2 Mozzarella cheese
- corn tortillas

- refried beans
- 2 cans black beans
- bag of white potatoes
- mushrooms
- pint each of raspberries and blueberries (buy frozen if out of season)
- grapes
- mango
- 2 peaches
- 2 red bell peppers, 1 green bell pepper
- celery
- cucumbers
- chili powder (the enchilada recipe calls for ½ cup, so stock up!)
- chicken thighs
- oatmeal
- maple syrup
- natural peanut

butter

- 2 cartons
chicken broth

- bag of carrots

- bag of onions

Breakfast:

- Bacon, egg and potato skillet

- Egg-in-a-hole and fruit

- Oatmeal with maple syrup and milk

- Mexican breakfast tortillas

- Berry yogurt breakfast cup and whole grain toast

Lunch:

- Easy pizza (buy a pre-made crust that has mozzarella cheese and sauce or what other ingredients you like) , fruit in the butter, add rice, water and 1 tsp. Cajun seasoning. Cook

- Easy black bean soup. Serve with shredded cheese and sour cream

- Black eyed peas and Cajun rice (sauté bell pepper, celery and diced onions)

- Tuna salad sandwiches (mix tuna with celery, pickle and diced onions) Add mayo, pepper, salt with carrot sticks and celery

- Peach Peanut Butter surprise sandwiches - Make an ordinary peanut butter sandwich, but

instead of jelly add thinly sliced ripe peaches, drizzle with honey .

Dinner:

- Chicken Gruy ere (or Swiss cheese) with green beans and herbed roasted new potatoes

- Salmon with Blueberry Grape Salad, rolls or croissants

- Cheese Enchiladas with Red Sauce served with sliced avocado and tomatoes, black olives, and sour cream

- Green Chiles Tortilla Casserole with avocado, cucumber salad and tomato

- Slow Cooker Corn Chowder with Shrimp and croissants

- Easy Slow Cooker Arroz con Pollo served with mango or other seasonal fruit

- Cheddar Potato Veggie Soup and whole grain bread

	Breakfast	Lunch	Dinner
M O N D A Y	Fresh Fruit and Cinnamon Oat Squares Pack an **Oat Square** and a piece of fruit for a quick breakfast to start the week.	Lentil Chili and Apple-Spinach Salad Thaw **Lentil Chili**. Make a big salad that consists of baby spinach, carrots, radishes and red onion. Remember to top it with healthy salad dressing.	Lentil Chili and Salad with Orange Peanut Dressing Combine Lentil Chili with a salad made of chopped broccoli florets, celery, carrots, roasted sweet potato and romaine. Toss the salad with some Orange Peanut Dressing and serve
T U E S D A	Loaded English Muffins and Fruit Salad Cook a bunch of greens with half a pint of halved cherry tomatoes. Use a	Green Pea Guacamole Wrap and Fresh Fruit Make a batch of Green Pea Guacamole. Spread whole grain tortillas with guacamole and add slices of	**Veggie Chili Enchiladas with salad and Chard** Make a burrito consisting with brown rice, chili and other ingredients. Warm half a bunch of bite-sized

Y	spoonful of this over whole English muffins. Top it with feta crumbles. Add fresh fruit on the side.	cucumber, radishes and toasted carrots on top. Roll up whole grain and serve with fresh fruit on the side.	cut chard as burrito is steaming then season chard with a non-fat condiment like vinegar or mild salsa. Add the green salad.
WEDNESDAY	Hot Cereal with Dried Fruit and Nuts Cook 2 servings of hot whole grain cereal according to the directions on the package. Top each serving with 1 tbsp each of raisins and walnuts.	**Black Bean Soup with Muffin and Salad** Heat the black bean soup and warm (if desired) the cornbread muffin. For the salad mixture, combine chopped carrots, celery, red or yellow bell pepper and other greens. Add organic dressing.	**Chili Baked Potato with Chard** Warm the chili and prepare the potato. Steam half a bunch of chopped, bite-size chard and season with a non-fat condiment of your choice. Add a green salad with organic dressing.
THURSDA	Apple-Cinnamon Oat Squares; Fresh Fruit Pack an **Oat Square** and a piece of fruit for a quick on-the-go	Tostadas with Salsa and Beans Put together refried beans, cheese and bake till warm. Top with salsa, sour cream and chopped avocado.	**Pasta with Tomatoes and Veggies + Salad** Prepare the sauce and boil the whole-wheat pasta. Serve with salad mixture and organic dressing. Save

Y	breakfast.		leftovers for later in the week.
F R I D A Y	**Quinoa Breakfast Bake and Fresh Fruit + Green Smoothie (optional)** Warm (if desired) quinoa bar and rinse fruit (slice or chop if needed). Consider blending a fresh-green filled shake with fresh greens if you prefer want something more filling.	**Cornbread Muffins and a Large Salad** Put together a big salad of green and colorful veggies Top with ingredients high in protein like tofu or beans. Use organic dressing. Warm cornbread muffin.	Tacos Serve with the following trimmings: avocados, shredded lettuce, shredded cheese, refried beans, ground beef, diced black olives, salsa, and sour cream.
S A T U	**Almond Rice Mighty Bowl +and Fruit Smoothie (optional)**	Garbanzo and Veggie-Stuffed Pitas with Fresh Fruit Drain a can of garbanzo beans and stir	Chicken (or baked tofu) with Rice + Salad Serve 3 ounces of cooked chicken with

R D A Y	Warm ½ cup brown rice in ½ cup of almond milk. Top with slices of banana + an ounce of chopped raw almonds, then Sweeten with chopped date. Blend smoothie with fresh fruits and ice.	together with ½ cup chopped avocado, 1 chopped cucumber, 4 chopped green onions, 2 cups shredded lettuce, and 1 shredded carrot. Drizzle with orange juice and tahini then stuff into the whole grain pitas. Serve fresh fruit for dessert.	half a cup of brown rice. Season with non-fat condiment of your choice, then add a large spinach salad with organic dressing.
S U N D A Y		Roasted Veggie and Hummus Wraps In a 400°F oven with parchment paper-lined baking sheet, roast 1 pound of mushrooms, 3 bell peppers and 2 quartered onions until brown and tender. Set this aside to cool then chop into bite-size pieces. Spread Homemade Hummus to whole grain tortillas and fill with veggies and roasted sweet potato. Store leftovers for use later.	Salmon and Wilted Greens over Quinoa with Roasted Sweet Potatoes Poach salmon in water and cook 5 cups of quinoa. Cook some spinach, frozen greens or Swiss Chard until just tender. Top combination with flaked salmon. Serve quinoa and roasted sweet potatoes on the side.

Product Recommendations

These are the top product brands to use based on my experience. Big savings on everyone's part, and better turnout with meals in general.

Barilla Whole Grain Rotini Pasta 13.25 Ounce Boxes (Pack of 4)

Price: $7.96 ($0.15 / oz)

Trimmed Asparagus

Description: 12 ounce package

Store: Trader Joe's

Price: $2.99

Marinated Artichokes

Description: 12 ounce jar (8.1 ounces drained weight)

Store: Trader Joe's

Price: $2.69

Shredded Mozzarella 16 ounce, resealable bag

Store: Trader Joe's

Price: $3.99

Hodgson Mill All Natural whole wheat whole grain lasagna pasta, 8 oz Box

Price: $2.24 ($0.22 / oz) + $4.99 shipping

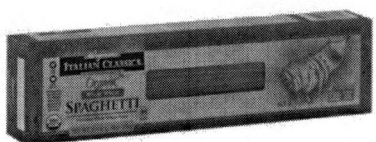

Wegmans Italian Classics Spaghetti, Organic, Whole Wheat, No. 4, 16 oz.

Store: Wegmans

Price: $2.49

Bob's Red Mill Millet Flour, Stone Ground, Whole Grain 23 oz.

Store: Wegmans

Price: $2.99

Bob's Red Mill Brown Rice Flour, Stone Ground, Whole Grain 24 oz.

Store: Wegmans

Price: $3.29

Bob's Red Mill Steel Cut Oats 24 oz. Bag, 1.50 lbs.

Store: Bob's Red Mill

Price: $3.19

Bob's Red Mill Organic Whole Oat Groats 29 oz. Bag, 1.81 lbs

Store: Bob's Red Mill

Price: **$3.69**

Native Forest Organic Coconut Milk -- 13.5 fl oz

Store: Amazon

Price: $2.49

Westsoy Organic Unsweetened Soymilk -- 32 fl oz

Store: Vitacost

Price: $3.69

Oak Farms Whole Milk Gallon

Store: The Milk Pail

Price: $5.58

Organic Valley Milk, Whole, Organic, 64 fl. oz.

Store: Wegmans

Price: $4.49

Muir Glen Organic Tomato Sauce, No Salt Added

Store: Wegmans

Price: $1.79

Organic Valley Family of Farms Heavy Whipping Cream, Organic, 16 fl. oz.

Store: Wegmans

Price: $3.99

Organic Valley Sour Cream, Organic, 16 oz.

Store: Wegmans

Price: $3.99

Organic Valley Organic Cheese, Raw Sharp Cheddar, 8 oz.

Store: Wegmans

Price: $5.69

Organic Valley Organic Parmesan Cheese, Shredded, 4 oz.

Store: Wegmans

Price: $4.99

Wegmans Organic Food You Feel Good About 85% Lean / 15% Fat Ground Beef Patties

Store: Wegmans

Price: $6.49

Wegmans Organic Food You Feel Good About Ground Beef, 93% Lean/7% Fat, FAMILY PACK, 48 oz.

Store: Wegmans

Price: **$15.57**

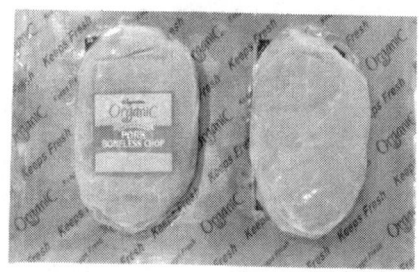

Wegmans Organic Food You Feel Good About Boneless Pork Chops

Store: Wegmans

Price: $8.99 / lb.

Budget-Friendly Whole Food Recipes

We are now in the last portion of the book, and before saying goodbye, I want to share to you some of my best recipes when preparing whole foods on a budget. I guarantee that these recipes will serve very useful and efficient as you transition your way towards achieving your goal weight without putting a strain in your pocket. Happy dieting!

BREAKFAST

1. WHOLE WHEAT HONEY BREAD

Servings: 12

Preparation time: 5 minutes

Cook time: 3 hours

Ready In: 3 hours and 5 minutes (using Bread Machine)/ 2 hours and 30 minutes (without Bread Machine)

Nutrition Facts

Serving Size 47 g

Amount Per Serving

Calories 173   Calories from Fat 20

	% Daily Value*
Total Fat 2.2g	**3%**
Saturated Fat 1.3g	**6%**
Trans Fat 0.0g	
Cholesterol 4mg	**1%**
Sodium 250mg	**10%**
Potassium 49mg	**1%**
Total Carbohydrates 32.7g	**11%**
Dietary Fiber 1.0g	**4%**
Sugars 8.2g	
Protein 5.8g	

Vitamin A 1%	•	Vitamin C 0%
Calcium 1%	•	Iron 9%

Nutrition Grade B

* Based on a 2000 calorie diet

Ingredients:

- 3 cups whole wheat flour
- 3 tablespoons vital wheat gluten
- 1 tablespoon dry milk powder
- 1 1/2 teaspoons active dry yeast
- 1 1/8 cups water (around 120 degrees F)
- 1 1/2 teaspoons sea salt
- 1/3 cup raw honey
- 1 1/2 tablespoons unsalted butter
- 1 pinch of brown sugar (if not using bread machine)
- 1 teaspoon coconut oil (for greasing, if not using bread machine)

Directions:

Using Bread Machine:
1. **Mix** the whole wheat flour, vital wheat gluten, milk powder, and yeast in a medium bowl. In another bowl, stir together the water, salt, honey, and butter.
2. **Place** both mixtures in bread machine pan in the order indicated by the manufacturer. Select Basic setting, then set the crust color to "Light" and then press Start.

Without Bread Machine:
1. **Mix** the water, yeast, and sugar in a large bowl. Allow to sit until foamy (about 10 minutes).
2. **Add** the remaining ingredients to the yeast mixture. Knead dough on a lightly floured surface until smooth, about 5-10 minutes.
3. **Transfer** the dough into a bowl greased with coconut oil and turn to coat. Cover and let the dough rise for 1 hour or until the dough has doubled in volume.
4. **Preheat** oven to 350 degrees F (175 degrees C). Knead dough again for 5 minutes.
5. **Place** the dough into a 9x5 inch loaf pan and let rise for 30 minutes.
6. **Bake** for 30 minutes in a preheated oven.

2. GINGER CHICKEN CONGEE

Servings: 4

Preparation time: 10 minutes

Cook time: 2 hours

Ready in: 2 hours 10 minutes

Nutrition Facts

Serving Size 279 g

Amount Per Serving

Calories 401	Calories from Fat 128

	% Daily Value*
Total Fat 14.2g	**22%**
Saturated Fat 3.9g	**19%**
Trans Fat 0.0g	
Cholesterol 168mg	**56%**
Sodium 322mg	**13%**
Potassium 521mg	**15%**
Total Carbohydrates 9.4g	**3%**
Dietary Fiber 1.3g	**5%**
Sugars 1.0g	
Protein 55.8g	

Vitamin A 6%	•	Vitamin C 9%
Calcium 3%	•	Iron 16%

Nutrition Grade B

* Based on a 2000 calorie diet

Ingredients:

- 1 (2.5 pound) whole chicken
- 3 (2 inch) pieces fresh ginger root
- 1 1/2 stalk lemon grass, chopped
- 1 tablespoon sea salt, or to taste
- 1/4 cup uncooked jasmine rice
- 1 cup low-sodium vegetable stock
- 1 medium carrot, diced
- Sea salt to taste
- 1 pinch ground black pepper to taste
- 1/4 cup chopped cilantro
- 1/8 cup chopped fresh chives
- 1/8 cup sautéed mushroom
- 1 lime, cut into 8 wedges

Directions:

1. **Place** chicken in a stock pot and cover with enough water. Add ginger, salt, and lemon grass; bring to a boil over medium-high heat. Reduce heat to medium-low and simmer, stirring occasionally, for 1 to 1 1/2 hours.
2. **Transfer** chicken to a cutting board and let cool. Shred the chicken to bite-size pieces then remove bones and skin; set aside.
3. **Stir** rice into broth, and bring to a boil. Reduce heat to medium, and then stir in the carrots and vegetable stock. Cook for 30 minutes, stirring occasionally. Return the chicken shreds to the pot and season with salt and pepper as needed.
4. **Ladle** congee into bowls, and top with cilantro, chives, and mushroom. Squeeze lime juice to taste.

3. SPINACH AND MUSHROOM FRITTATA

Servings: 6

Preparation time: 10 minutes

Cook time: 40 minutes

Ready in: 50 minutes

Nutrition Facts

Serving Size 174 g

Amount Per Serving

Calories 195	Calories from Fat 98

% Daily Value*

Total Fat 10.9g	**17%**
Saturated Fat 4.4g	**22%**
Trans Fat 0.0g	
Cholesterol 150mg	**50%**
Sodium 675mg	**28%**
Potassium 373mg	**11%**
Total Carbohydrates 5.2g	**2%**
Dietary Fiber 1.3g	**5%**
Sugars 1.2g	
Protein 19.9g	

Vitamin A 96%	Vitamin C 26%
Calcium 21%	Iron 15%

Nutrition Grade B+

* Based on a 2000 calorie diet

Ingredients:

- 3/4 cup chopped Portobello mushrooms
- 1 medium shallot, chopped
- 1/2 cup finely chopped scallions with some green tops
- 1 (10 ounce) package frozen chopped spinach, thawed
- 4 eggs
- 1 cup cottage cheese
- 3/4 cup freshly grated Parmesan cheese
- 1/4 teaspoon sea salt
- 1 pinch pepper, to taste
- 1/8 teaspoon dried rosemary
- 1/8 teaspoon dried thyme
- Coconut oil or olive oil for greasing

Directions:

1. **Preheat** oven to 375 degrees. Grease a 9-inch pie plate with coconut or olive oil.
2. **Sauté** the mushrooms and shallot in olive or coconut oil in a skillet over medium-high heat until mushroom is lightly browned.
3. **Transfer** sautéed mushroom and shallot into a large bowl. Add the remaining ingredients and whisk together until well blended. Place the spinach mixture into the prepared pie plate.
4. **Bake** for 30 minutes, or until browned and set. Let cool then cut in wedges and serve.

4. BREAKFAST BURRITO

Servings: 4

Preparation time: 25 minutes

Cook time: 13 minutes

Ready in: 38 minutes

Nutrition Facts

Serving Size 301 g

Amount Per Serving

Calories 331 — Calories from Fat 185

	% Daily Value*
Total Fat 20.6g	**32%**
Saturated Fat 5.9g	**29%**
Trans Fat 0.0g	
Cholesterol 174mg	**58%**
Sodium 504mg	**21%**
Potassium 726mg	**21%**
Total Carbohydrates 24.2g	**8%**
Dietary Fiber 7.3g	**29%**
Sugars 5.7g	
Protein 15.2g	

Vitamin A 37%	•	Vitamin C 90%
Calcium 13%	•	Iron 14%

Nutrition Grade A-

* Based on a 2000 calorie diet

Ingredients:

- 2 teaspoons olive oil, plus more for greasing the skillet
- 1 cup diced red onion
- 1 red bell pepper, seeded and diced
- 1/4 teaspoon red pepper flakes
- Sea salt and freshly ground black pepper to taste
- 4 organic eggs and 4 organic egg whites
- 1/3 cup shredded Cheddar cheese
- 4 (10-inch) whole-wheat tortillas (burrito-size)
- 1/2 cup salsa (ingredients below)
- 1 large tomato, seeded and diced
- 1 small avocado, cubed
- 2 tablespoons chopped fresh cilantro

For the salsa:

- 1 cup diced tomatoes
- 1 small shallot, chopped
- 1 Serrano chili pepper, seeded
- 1 clove garlic, peeled
- 1/2 lime, juiced
- sea salt and pepper to taste
- 1/2 teaspoon extra-virgin olive oil

Directions:

1. **Prepare** the salsa: Place the tomatoes, shallot, chilli pepper, garlic, and lime juice in a food processor and pulse until finely chopped. Season with salt and pepper to taste. Drizzle with olive oil. Cover and refrigerate.
2. **Heat** the olive oil in a large skillet over a medium-high heat. Add the onions and peppers, and sauté until onions are translucent, about 5 minutes. Add red pepper flakes and season with salt and pepper to taste.

3. **Grease** the skillet with olive oil, and place over medium heat. Beat together the eggs and egg whites then stir in the cheese. Reduce heat to low and pour the egg mixture into the skillet, stirring and turning until cooked through, about 3 minutes.
4. **Spread** each tortilla with 2 tablespoons of the prepared salsa, and then layer with 1/4 of the scrambled eggs, 2 tablespoons diced tomato and 1/4 of the avocado. Sprinkle with some cilantro, then roll up and serve.

5. GOLDEN SCOTCH EGGS

Servings: 8

Preparation time: 20 minutes

Cook time: 25 minutes

Ready In: 45 minutes

Nutrition Facts

Serving Size 193 g

Amount Per Serving

Calories 392	Calories from Fat 208
	% Daily Value*
Total Fat 23.1g	**35%**
Saturated Fat 5.3g	**27%**
Trans Fat 0.0g	
Cholesterol 184mg	**61%**
Sodium 799mg	**33%**
Potassium 207mg	**6%**
Total Carbohydrates 14.2g	**5%**
Dietary Fiber 4.0g	**16%**
Protein 32.7g	

Vitamin A 5%	•	Vitamin C 2%
Calcium 9%	•	Iron 14%

Nutrition Grade B-

* Based on a 2000 calorie diet

Ingredients:

- 8 eggs
- 2 pounds lean ground pork
- 1 bunch fresh sage, chopped
- 6 tablespoons fennel seeds
- 1 tablespoon sea salt
- 2 teaspoons ground black pepper
- 1 cup whole grain flour
- 1/2 cup extra-virgin olive oil or coconut oil
- Sliced tomatoes and mustard for garnish (optional)

Directions:

1. **Preheat** oven to 350 degrees F (175 degrees C). Heat oil in deep-fryer to 375 degrees F (190 degrees C).
2. **Boil** the eggs in a pot or saucepan. Let the eggs cool in ice water for about 10 minutes. When cooled, peel the eggs and set aside.
3. **Combine** the ground pork, sage, fennel seeds, salt, and pepper in a large bowl. Form patties with the pork mixture and wrap around each boiled egg. Lightly flour each coated egg.
4. **Coat** the bottom of a deep pan with the oil then heat for 2 minutes over high heat. Pan-fry the eggs in batches, turning occasionally to brown all sides. Transfer eggs to the preheated oven and bake for 10 minutes.
5. **Cut** eggs in half, and serve with sliced tomatoes and mustard if desired.

6. BROWN RICE PORRIDGE WITH FRUITS AND NUTS

Servings: 2

Preparation time: 5 minutes

Cook time: 25 minutes

Ready In: 30 minutes

Nutrition Facts

Serving Size 253 g

Amount Per Serving

Calories 692	Calories from Fat 301

% Daily Value*

Total Fat 33.4g	**51%**
Saturated Fat 26.2g	**131%**
Trans Fat 0.0g	
Cholesterol 0mg	**0%**
Sodium 168mg	**7%**
Potassium 629mg	**18%**
Total Carbohydrates 91.9g	**31%**
Dietary Fiber 7.0g	**28%**
Sugars 15.0g	
Protein 10.7g	

Vitamin A 0%	•	Vitamin C 11%
Calcium 6%	•	Iron 22%

Nutrition Grade C

* Based on a 2000 calorie diet

Ingredients:
- 1 cup coconut milk or soy milk
- 2 tablespoons mixture of dried fruits or frozen berries
- 1/4 cup chopped apples
- 1 tablespoon raw honey
- 1 dash cinnamon
- 1 cup cooked brown rice
- 1/4 teaspoon pure vanilla extract
- 1 pinch nutmeg
- 1 tablespoon toasted nuts
- 1 pinch sea salt

Directions:
1. Place the cooked brown rice, milk, fruits, honey, and cinnamon in a small saucepan. Mix and bring to a boil over medium heat. Reduce heat to low and simmer for 20 minutes.
2. Add the brown rice, vanilla, nutmeg, nuts, and salt; stir until well blended. Cook for additional 2 minutes, or until thick.

7. BACON N' MUSHROOM OMELETTE

Servings: 3

Preparation time: 10 minutes

Cook time: 35 minutes

Ready in: 45 minutes

Nutrition Facts

Serving Size 202 g

Amount Per Serving

Calories 370   Calories from Fat 244

	% Daily Value*
Total Fat 27.1g	**42%**
Saturated Fat 11.9g	**60%**
Trans Fat 0.0g	
Cholesterol 247mg	**82%**
Sodium 1426mg	**59%**
Potassium 382mg	**11%**
Total Carbohydrates 6.9g	**2%**
Dietary Fiber 1.8g	**7%**
Sugars 3.7g	
Protein 24.0g	

Vitamin A 35%	•	Vitamin C 74%
Calcium 20%	•	Iron 12%

Nutrition Grade C

* Based on a 2000 calorie diet

Ingredients:

- 1/4 pound bacon, cut crosswise in 1-inch slices
- 1 tablespoon unsalted butter (or extra-virgin olive oil)
- 1 cup sliced Portobello mushrooms
- 1/2 cup chopped yellow onion
- 1 medium red bell pepper, diced
- 1 fresh tomato, chopped
- 4 extra-large eggs
- 2 tablespoons whole fat organic milk
- 3/4 teaspoon sea salt
- 1/2 teaspoon freshly ground black pepper
- 1/4 cup chopped chives
- 3 ounces extra-sharp Cheddar cheese, shredded, more for garnish

Directions:

1. **Preheat** the oven to 350 degrees F.
2. **Cook** the bacon in a pan over medium-low heat until

browned, about 5 minutes. Drain the bacon on paper towels and discard excess fat from pan; set aside.

3. **Melt** the butter in the same pan over medium-low heat, and then stir in the mushrooms, yellow onion, red bell pepper, and tomato. Cook for about 10 minutes, stirring occasionally, until the mushroom is tender.

4. **While** the vegetables are cooking, beat together the eggs, milk, salt, and pepper in a medium bowl. Stir in the chives and cheese.

5. **Add** the cooked bacon to the vegetables in the pan and pour over the egg mixture. Place the pan in the preheated oven for 20 to 25 minutes, or until the eggs are almost done in the center.

6. **Sprinkle** with grated cheese on top and bake for another minute. Serve warm.

8. QUINOA PORRIDGE

Servings: 3

Preparation time: 5 minutes

Cook time: 30 minutes

Ready In: 35 minutes

Nutrition Facts

Serving Size 160 g

Amount Per Serving

Calories 201   Calories from Fat 34

	% Daily Value*
Total Fat 3.8g	**6%**
Trans Fat 0.0g	
Cholesterol 0mg	**0%**
Sodium 144mg	**6%**
Potassium 328mg	**9%**
Total Carbohydrates 33.4g	**11%**
Dietary Fiber 2.8g	**11%**
Sugars 12.7g	
Protein 7.9g	

Vitamin A 0%	•	Vitamin C 0%
Calcium 5%	•	Iron 12%

Nutrition Grade B-

* Based on a 2000 calorie diet

Ingredients:

- 1/2 cup quinoa
- 1/4 teaspoon ground cinnamon
- 1 1/2 cups soy milk
- 2 tablespoons raw brown sugar (or 1 1/2 tablespoons agave nectar)
- 1 teaspoon vanilla extract (optional)
- 1 pinch sea salt
- 1 tablespoon raisins for topping (optional)

Directions:

1. **Heat** a saucepan over medium heat and measure in the quinoa. Season with cinnamon and cook until toasted, stirring frequently, about 3 minutes.
2. **Stir** in the soy milk, brown sugar, vanilla, and salt. Bring mixture to a boil over medium-high heat.

3. **Reduce** heat to low. Cover and simmer porridge for about 25 minutes, or until the grains are tender. Add more milk or water if needed. Stir occasionally and let the extra liquid cook off until a desired consistency is reached.
4. **Serve** topped with raisins or any of your favourite fruits and nuts.

9. APPLE CINNAMON PEANUT BUTTER SANDWICH

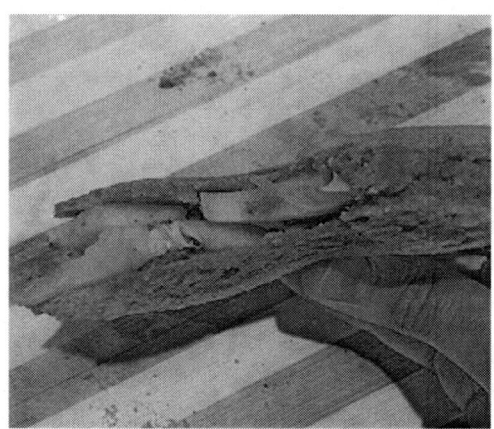

Servings: 4

Ready in: 10 minutes

Nutrition Facts

Serving Size 153 g

Amount Per Serving

Calories 425	Calories from Fat 153

	% Daily Value*
Total Fat 17.0g	**26%**
Saturated Fat 3.0g	**15%**
Trans Fat 0.0g	
Cholesterol 0mg	**0%**
Sodium 257mg	**11%**
Potassium 46mg	**1%**
Total Carbohydrates 50.1g	**17%**
Dietary Fiber 13.2g	**53%**
Sugars 18.3g	
Protein 18.0g	

Vitamin A 0%	•	Vitamin C 5%
Calcium 21%	•	Iron 40%

Nutrition Grade B-

* Based on a 2000 calorie diet

Ingredients:

- 1/2 cup natural peanut butter
- 1 teaspoon ground cinnamon
- 1 1/2 tablespoons honey
- 1 small apple, sliced thinly
- 8 slices whole-grain bread

Directions:

1. Mix together the peanut butter, cinnamon, and honey in a small bowl.
2. Spread 2 tablespoons of the peanut butter mixture on each of the 4 slices of bread. Add apple slices on top then cover with the remaining bread slices.

10. BANANA CORNBREAD WITH ALMONDS

Servings: 8

Preparation time: 10 minutes

Cook time: 40 minutes

Ready in: 50 minutes

Nutrition Facts

Serving Size 121 g

Amount Per Serving

Calories 350	Calories from Fat 154

% Daily Value*

Total Fat 17.1g	**26%**
Saturated Fat 7.0g	**35%**
Trans Fat 0.0g	
Cholesterol 2mg	**1%**
Sodium 292mg	**12%**
Potassium 514mg	**15%**
Total Carbohydrates 43.4g	**14%**
Dietary Fiber 6.7g	**27%**
Sugars 10.7g	
Protein 7.3g	

Vitamin A 1%	•	Vitamin C 7%
Calcium 16%	•	Iron 12%

Nutrition Grade C-

* Based on a 2000 calorie diet

Ingredients:

- 2 tablespoons pure maple syrup
- 3 bananas, mashed
- 1/2 cup organic whole milk
- 1/4 cup extra-virgin coconut oil, plus extra for greasing pan
- 1/4 cup applesauce
- 2 teaspoons vanilla extract
- 1 cup whole cornmeal
- 1 cup whole wheat flour
- 1 teaspoon baking soda
- 1 tablespoon baking powder
- 1/2 teaspoon cinnamon
- 1/2 teaspoon sea salt
- 1 1/2 cups sliced almonds

Directions:

1. **Preheat** oven to 350 degrees F (175 degrees C). Grease an 8x8 inch baking pan with coconut oil.
2. **Place** the maple syrup, mashed bananas, milk, coconut oil, applesauce, and vanilla into a food processor or blender; process until combined and smooth.
3. **Sift** together the cornmeal, flour, baking soda, baking powder, cinnamon, and salt in a bowl. Add the flour mixture into the banana mixture and stir until combined.
4. **Fold** in the sliced bananas, and 1 cup of the sliced almonds. Pour mixture into the prepared pan, and then spread the remaining almond slices on top.
5. **Bake** for 40 minutes, or until golden brown on top.

11. MULTI-GRAIN BLUEBERRY PANCAKES

Servings: 4

Prep Time: 15 Minutes

Cook Time: 15 Minutes

Ready In: 30 Minutes

Nutrition Facts

Serving Size 230 g

Amount Per Serving

Calories 360	Calories from Fat 60

	% Daily Value*
Total Fat 6.6g	**10%**
Saturated Fat 2.8g	**14%**
Cholesterol 56mg	**19%**
Sodium 549mg	**23%**
Potassium 674mg	**19%**
Total Carbohydrates 64.4g	**21%**
Dietary Fiber 4.4g	**18%**
Sugars 18.5g	
Protein 12.1g	

Vitamin A 4%	•	Vitamin C 11%
Calcium 34%	•	Iron 33%

Nutrition Grade B-

* Based on a 2000 calorie diet

Ingredients:

- 1 cup rolled oats
- 1 cup whole wheat flour
- 1/4 cup whole cornmeal
- 1 teaspoon vanilla extract
- 3 tablespoons molasses/ raw honey
- 1 teaspoon baking powder
- 1/2 teaspoon baking soda
- 1/2 teaspoon sea salt
- 1 egg, beaten
- 1 3/4 cups whole buttermilk
- 1 cup fresh blueberries
- olive oil or coconut oil for greasing the griddle

Directions:

1. **Mix** the oats, whole wheat flour, cornmeal, vanilla, molasses, baking powder, baking soda, and salt in a large bowl. Add the egg and buttermilk; stir until mixture is well blended. Let the batter sit for 15 minutes then fold in the blueberries.
2. **Grease** a large skillet or griddle with oil and place over medium heat. Add about ¼ cup of batter onto the griddle. Flip the pancake once bubbles burst; continue cooking until browned on the other side. Repeat with remaining batter.
3. **Serve** with maple syrup or honey.

12. BEEF CASSEROLE

Servings: 6

Preparation time: 10 minutes

Cook time: 30 minutes

Ready in: 40 minutes

Nutrition Facts

Serving Size 169 g

Amount Per Serving

Calories 309	Calories from Fat 168

	% Daily Value*
Total Fat 18.6g	**29%**
Saturated Fat 7.3g	**37%**
Cholesterol 196mg	**65%**
Sodium 524mg	**22%**
Potassium 474mg	**14%**
Total Carbohydrates 2.8g	**1%**
Sugars 0.9g	
Protein 32.0g	

Vitamin A 11%	•	Vitamin C 13%
Calcium 16%	•	Iron 84%

Nutrition Grade B

* Based on a 2000 calorie diet

Ingredients:

- 1 pound lean ground beef
- 2 shallots, diced
- 3 cloves of garlic, minced
- 1 medium zucchini, peeled and shredded
- 4 eggs
- 2 tablespoon snipped parsley
- 1 tablespoon fresh basil, minced
- Sea salt and pepper, to taste
- 1 cup shredded organic cheddar cheese
- 2 tablespoons extra-virgin olive oil, plus extra for greasing

Directions:

1. **Preheat** oven to 350 degrees F. Grease a 9×13 inch baking dish with olive oil.
2. **Place** a medium skillet over medium heat. Add the beef, shallots, and garlic; cook until beef is crumbly. Set aside.
3. **Heat** 2 tablespoons olive oil in another skillet over medium heat. Add the zucchini and sauté until tender. Transfer to a bowl and set aside.
4. **Beat** together the eggs, parsley, and basil in a large bowl. Add cooked beef and season with salt and pepper. Pour mixture into the prepared baking dish then sprinkle with the cheese.
5. **Cook** in the preheated oven for 30 minutes or until a toothpick inserted into the center of the casserole comes out clean. Slice and serve.

13. GREEN SMOOTHIE

Servings: 4

Ready in: 10 minutes

Nutrition Facts

Serving Size 214 g

Amount Per Serving

Calories 250   Calories from Fat 92

% Daily Value*

Total Fat 10.3g	**16%**
Saturated Fat 9.0g	**45%**
Trans Fat 0.0g	
Cholesterol 0mg	**0%**
Sodium 26mg	**1%**
Potassium 586mg	**17%**
Total Carbohydrates 41.6g	**14%**
Dietary Fiber 6.5g	**26%**
Sugars 29.8g	
Protein 2.6g	

Vitamin A 44%	•	Vitamin C 31%
Calcium 4%	•	Iron 29%

Nutrition Grade B+

* Based on a 2000 calorie diet

Ingredients

- 2 bananas, sliced in chunks
- 2 cups seedless grapes (or berries)
- 1 ½ cup coconut or soy milk
- 2 tablespoons raw honey
- 1 apple, cored and chopped
- 3 cups fresh spinach or kale leaves
- 1 cup crushed ice

Directions :

Place all ingredients into a blender and process until your desired consistency is reached. Serve in glasses.

14. JUMP START GRANOLA

Servings: 10

Preparation time: 15 minutes

Cook time: 20 minutes

Ready in: 35 minutes

Nutrition Facts

Serving Size 81 g

Amount Per Serving

Calories 337   Calories from Fat 133

	% Daily Value*
Total Fat 14.8g	**23%**
Saturated Fat 2.7g	**14%**
Trans Fat 0.0g	
Cholesterol 0mg	**0%**
Sodium 25mg	**1%**
Potassium 177mg	**5%**
Total Carbohydrates 48.8g	**16%**
Dietary Fiber 5.0g	**20%**
Sugars 15.1g	
Protein 6.1g	

Vitamin A 0%	•	Vitamin C 0%
Calcium 2%	•	Iron 4%

Nutrition Grade C+

* Based on a 2000 calorie diet

Ingredients

- 3 cups whole rolled oats
- 1 cup chopped nut, use any of your favourite (such as almonds, pecans, walnuts, etc.)
- 1 cup of your favourite seeds (such as sunflower seeds, pumpkin seeds, flax seeds, etc.)
- 1/2 cup dried fruits (such as apricots, dates, cranberries, etc.)
- 1/2 cup raw honey or pure maple syrup
- 1 tablespoon coconut oil, plus extra for greasing pan
- 2 teaspoons ground cinnamon
- pinch of sea salt (optional)

Directions

1. **Preheat** oven to 300 degrees F (150 degrees C). Grease the bottom and sides of baking pan with coconut oil.
2. **Combine** oats, nuts, seeds, and dried fruits in a bowl.
3. **Mix** the honey, coconut oil, cinnamon and salt then stir into the oats mixture.
4. **Spread** mixture into the prepared baking pan.
5. **Bake** for 20 minutes, stirring halfway through.
6. **Let** cool completely before serving.

LUNCH

1. CHICKEN NOODLE SOUP

Servings: 5

Preparation time:

Cook time:

Ready in:

Nutrition Facts

Serving Size 439 g

Amount Per Serving

Calories 234   Calories from Fat 74

	% Daily Value*
Total Fat 8.3g	**13%**
Saturated Fat 4.4g	**22%**
Trans Fat 0.0g	
Cholesterol 65mg	**22%**
Sodium 934mg	**39%**
Potassium 129mg	**4%**
Total Carbohydrates 21.6g	**7%**
Dietary Fiber 2.8g	**11%**
Sugars 4.5g	
Protein 20.5g	

Vitamin A 9%	•	Vitamin C 8%
Calcium 2%	•	Iron 15%

Nutrition Grade C-

* Based on a 2000 calorie diet

Ingredients:

- 2 tablespoons real butter
- 1/2 cup chopped onion
- 1/2 cup chopped celery
- 2 cloves garlic, minced
- 2 cups chopped, cooked chicken meat
- 1 cup chopped carrots
- 48 oz. Organic low-sodium chicken broth
- 1/4 teaspoon dried basil
- 1/4 teaspoon ground black pepper
- 1 bay leaf
- 1/2 tablespoon dried cilantro
- 1/4 teaspoon oregano
- Sea salt to taste
- 4 ounces whole wheat egg noodles

Directions:

1. **Melt** butter in a large stock pot over medium heat. Add the celery, garlic, and onion; sauté until onion is translucent.
2. **Stir** in the chicken and carrots then cover with the chicken broth. Season with basil, black pepper, bay leaf, cilantro, oregano, and salt. Simmer for 30 minutes.
3. **Add** noodles, and cook for additional 10 minutes.

2. BEEF POT ROAST

Servings: 8

Preparation time: 15 minutes

Cook time: 3 hours 15 minutes

Ready in: 3 hours 30 minutes

Nutrition Facts

Serving Size 303 g

Amount Per Serving

Calories 777	Calories from Fat 494

	% Daily Value*
Total Fat 54.9g	**84%**
Saturated Fat 22.5g	**113%**
Trans Fat 0.0g	
Cholesterol 212mg	**71%**
Sodium 755mg	**31%**
Potassium 799mg	**23%**
Total Carbohydrates 12.0g	**4%**
Dietary Fiber 2.3g	**9%**
Sugars 2.2g	
Protein 55.8g	

Vitamin A 7%	•	Vitamin C 39%
Calcium 3%	•	Iron 38%

Nutrition Grade C+

* Based on a 2000 calorie diet

Ingredients:

- 3 1/2 pounds beef chuck pot roast
- 2 teaspoons salt
- 1 teaspoon ground black pepper
- 1 tablespoon olive oil
- 1 large carrot, cut into big chunks
- 2 medium potatoes, cut into big chunks
- 2 cloves garlic
- 1 cup diced green peppers
- 1 cup diced onion
- 1/4 cup butter
- 1 teaspoon dried coriander
- 1 pinch celery seed (optional)

Directions:

1. **Preheat** the oven to 275 degrees F (135 degrees C). Rub the chuck roast with salt and pepper.
2. **Heat** olive oil in a large oven-safe pot over medium-high heat. Add the meat and brown on both sides. Transfer to a plate and set aside.
3. **Add** the carrots, potatoes, garlic, green peppers, and onion into the pot, and cook for about 3 minutes or until the onions are translucent. Add butter and cook for 5 minutes more. Stir in the coriander and celery seed. Return the roast to the pot then cover pot with the lid.
4. **Roast** in the preheated oven for about 2 1/2 to 3 hours, or until tender.

3. TACO SALAD WITH RANCH DRESSING

Servings: 6

Preparation time: 30 minutes

Cook time: 15 minutes

Ready in: 45 minutes

Nutrition Facts

Serving Size 378 g

Amount Per Serving

Calories 551	Calories from Fat 167

	% Daily Value*
Total Fat 18.5g	**29%**
Saturated Fat 5.3g	**26%**
Trans Fat 0.0g	
Cholesterol 85mg	**28%**
Sodium 870mg	**36%**
Potassium 1058mg	**30%**
Total Carbohydrates 58.1g	**19%**
Dietary Fiber 10.2g	**41%**
Sugars 7.5g	
Protein 39.1g	

Vitamin A 35%	•	Vitamin C 26%
Calcium 19%	•	Iron 107%

Nutrition Grade A-

* Based on a 2000 calorie diet

Ingredients:
- 1 pound lean ground beef
- 1 tablespoon chili powder
- 1/4 teaspoon garlic powder
- 1/4 teaspoon onion powder
- Sea salt and ground black pepper to taste
- 1 head iceberg lettuce, shredded
- 2 ripe tomatoes, diced
- 1/2 cup shredded cheddar cheese
- 1 cup organic kidney beans
- 1 large onion, diced
- 1 cup ranch dressing (recipe below)
- 1 cup low-sodium salsa
- Whole Wheat Tortilla Chips, to serve

Ranch dressing:
- 2/3 cup mayonnaise
- 1/4 cup plain yogurt
- 1 finely chopped fresh dill weed
- 1/4 teaspoon garlic powder
- 1/8 teaspoon onion powder
- 1 pinch sea salt
- 1 pinch ground black pepper

Directions:

1. **Whisk** together all the ingredients for the ranch dressing in a bowl. Refrigerate in a sealed container for at least 30 minutes before serving.
2. **Place** a heavy skillet over medium-high heat. Add the ground beef and cook until browned, about 10 minutes. Drain excess fat. Season with chili powder, garlic powder, onion powder, salt, and pepper. Set aside.
3. **Toss** together the lettuce, browned beef, tomatoes, cheese, beans, and onions in a large bowl. Drizzle with the prepared ranch dressing; toss well to combine. Serve with salsa and tortilla chips.

4. BLACK BEAN CHILI

Servings: 4

Preparation time: 20 minutes

Cook time: 20 minutes

Ready in: 40 minutes

Nutrition Facts

Serving Size 406 g

Amount Per Serving

Calories 489	Calories from Fat 85

	% Daily Value*
Total Fat 9.4g	**14%**
Saturated Fat 2.9g	**15%**
Cholesterol 6mg	**2%**
Sodium 448mg	**19%**
Potassium 1850mg	**53%**
Total Carbohydrates 79.9g	**27%**
Dietary Fiber 18.6g	**74%**
Sugars 11.9g	
Protein 25.3g	

Vitamin A 43%	•	Vitamin C 124%
Calcium 16%	•	Iron 35%

Nutrition Grade A

* Based on a 2000 calorie diet

Ingredients:

- 2 cups dry black beans, rinsed
- 1 tablespoon olive oil
- 2 cloves garlic, crushed and chopped
- 1 onion, chopped
- 1 red bell pepper, seeded and chopped
- 3 roma (plum) tomatoes, diced
- 1 medium zucchini, diced
- 1/2 cup fresh corn kernels
- 1/2 teaspoon sea salt
- 1/2 teaspoon ground black pepper
- 1/2 tablespoon red pepper flakes
- 1 cup organic chicken broth
- 1 medium red onion, chopped, for garnish (optional)
- 1/4 cup sour cream (optional)

Directions:

1. **Soak** black beans in cold water overnight. Drain beans and place in a large saucepan. Add fresh water enough to cover beans. Simmer over medium-high heat until tender, about 1 hour. Drain and set aside.

2. **Heat** olive oil in a large saucepan over medium-high heat. Add the garlic, onion, red bell peppers, tomatoes, zucchini, s and corn for 10 minutes or until the onions are translucent. Season with salt, black pepper, and red pepper flakes. Add the black beans and chicken broth, bring mixture to a boil.

3. **Pour** 1 cup of the soup to a food processor or blender; puree, pour back into the soup, and stir. Serve hot garnished with chopped onion and sour cream.

5. CHICKEN MEATBALL SOUP

Servings: 6

Preparation time: 15 minutes

Cook time: 45 minutes

Ready in: 1 hour

Nutrition Facts

Serving Size 512 g

Amount Per Serving

Calories 167　　　　　Calories from Fat 30

	% Daily Value*
Total Fat 3.4g	**5%**
Trans Fat 0.0g	
Cholesterol 47mg	**16%**
Sodium 455mg	**19%**
Potassium 284mg	**8%**
Total Carbohydrates 12.7g	**4%**
Dietary Fiber 2.8g	**11%**
Sugars 3.4g	
Protein 22.4g	

Vitamin A 9%	Vitamin C 20%
Calcium 3%	Iron 7%

Nutrition Grade B+

* Based on a 2000 calorie diet

Ingredients:

For the Meatballs:
- 1 pound ground chicken breast
- 1 cup chopped onion
- 3 cloves garlic, crushed and chopped
- 1/2 cup whole wheat bread crumbs
- 1/2 teaspoon ground black pepper
- 1/2 teaspoon sea salt

For the Soup:
- 1 tablespoon olive oil, plus extra for greasing baking sheet
- 1 1/2 teaspoons minced garlic
- 1 1/2 cups chopped celery
- 1 1/2 cups sliced zucchini
- 1 1/2 cups sliced carrots
- 4 cups water
- 4 cups low-sodium chicken broth
- 1/2 teaspoon sea salt
- 1/2 teaspoon ground black pepper
- 1 bay leaf

Directions:

1. **Preheat** oven to 400 degrees F (205 degrees C). Lightly grease a baking sheet with olive oil.
2. **Combine** the chicken, 1/2 cup chopped onion, garlic, bread crumbs, pepper, and salt in a large bowl. Using wet hands, form mixture into small meatballs. Place them on the prepared baking sheet.
3. **Bake** in preheated oven for about 15 minutes. Drain meatballs in paper towels and set aside.
4. **Heat** 1 tablespoon olive oil in a large saucepan over medium heat. Add the garlic and remaining onions; sauté until onion is translucent. Add the celery, zucchini, and carrots; stir then cover with water and chicken broth. Season with salt and pepper to taste, and add the bay leaf. Bring to a boil over medium-high heat. Reduce heat to medium-low, and simmer for 15 to 20 minutes.
5. **Add** the meatballs and stir. Remove the bay leaf from soup and serve hot.

6. CRISPY FISH FILLETS

Servings: 4

Preparation time: 10 minutes

Cook time: 10 minutes

Ready in: 20 minutes

Nutrition Facts

Serving Size 242 g

Amount Per Serving

Calories 350	Calories from Fat 46

	% Daily Value*
Total Fat 5.1g	**8%**
Saturated Fat 2.6g	**13%**
Trans Fat 0.0g	
Cholesterol 124mg	**41%**
Sodium 225mg	**9%**
Potassium 97mg	**3%**
Total Carbohydrates 37.3g	**12%**
Dietary Fiber 2.0g	**8%**
Sugars 0.6g	
Protein 38.4g	

Vitamin A 1%	•	Vitamin C 1%
Calcium 5%	•	Iron 27%

Nutrition Grade B

* Based on a 2000 calorie diet

Ingredients:

- 1 1/2 cups whole wheat flour
- 1 organic egg
- 1 clove garlic, crushed and chopped
- 1/2 teaspoon chopped parsley
- 2 tablespoons organic Dijon mustard
- 1 dash sea salt
- 1/4 cup coconut or olive oil
- 4 (6 ounce) tilapia fillets

Directions:

1. **Place** the flour in a shallow dish. In another shallow dish, whisk together the egg, garlic, parsley, mustard, and salt.
2. **Heat** oil in a large skillet over medium-high heat.
3. **Dredge** the fish fillets in flour to coat, and then dip them in the egg mixture. Dredge the fillets in flour again.
4. **Fry** fish fillets for 2 minutes on each side, or until golden brown.

7. LEMON STEAMED FISH

Servings: 6

Preparation time: 15 minutes

Cook time: 30 minutes

Ready in: 45 minutes

Nutrition Facts

Serving Size 191 g

Amount Per Serving

Calories 169   Calories from Fat 36

	% Daily Value*
Total Fat 4.1g	**6%**
Cholesterol 84mg	**28%**
Sodium 148mg	**6%**
Potassium 51mg	**1%**
Total Carbohydrates 2.2g	**1%**
Sugars 0.5g	
Protein 30.7g	

Vitamin A 2%   •   Vitamin C 11%

Calcium 1%   •   Iron 2%

Nutrition Grade C+

* Based on a 2000 calorie diet

Ingredients:

- 6 (6 ounce) cod fillets
- 2 2-inch piece ginger, cut into matchsticks
- 1/4 cup chopped onion
- 1/4 teaspoon paprika
- sea salt to taste
- 2 clove garlic, minced
- 1 pinch ground black pepper
- 2 teaspoons dried parsley
- 1/4 cup fresh lemon juice
- 1 tablespoon extra-virgin olive oil
- Scallions cut into 1-inch strips, for garnish

Directions:

1. **Preheat** oven to 375 degrees F (190 degrees C).
2. **Make** 6 foil squares, large enough for the size of each fillet.
3. **Place** a fillet on the center of each foil square. Sprinkle each fillet with ginger, onion, paprika, salt, garlic, pepper, and parsley.
4. **Drizzle** lemon juice and olive oil over each fillet then loosely seal the foil, pleating seams to enclose. Place packets on a baking sheet.
5. **Bake** in the preheated oven for 30 minutes.
6. **Serve** steamed fillets garnished with scallions.

8. CHEDDAR PORK HAMBURGERS

Servings: 4

Preparation time: 5 minutes

Cook time: 15 minutes

Ready in: 20 minutes

Nutrition Facts

Serving Size 189 g

Amount Per Serving	
Calories 384	Calories from Fat 131
	% Daily Value*
Total Fat 14.6g	**22%**
Saturated Fat 6.3g	**31%**
Trans Fat 0.0g	
Cholesterol 157mg	**52%**
Sodium 611mg	**25%**
Potassium 606mg	**17%**
Total Carbohydrates 19.7g	**7%**
Dietary Fiber 2.9g	**12%**
Sugars 3.6g	
Protein 42.6g	
Vitamin A 4% • Vitamin C 1%	
Calcium 15% • Iron 126%	

Nutrition Grade B+

* Based on a 2000 calorie diet

Ingredients:
- 1 pound ground beef
- 1/2 cup shredded Cheddar cheese
- 1 organic egg
- 1/2 teaspoon salt
- 1/2 teaspoon pepper
- 1 teaspoon Worcestershire sauce
- 1 clove garlic, minced
- 4 whole wheat hamburger buns
- 4 lettuce leaves
- 4 cucumber slices

Directions:
1. **Preheat** grill for high heat.
2. **Combine** the ground beef, Cheddar cheese, egg, salt, pepper, Worcestershire sauce, and garlic in a large bowl. Form the mixture into 4 hamburger patties.
3. **Lightly** oil the grill grate. Place hamburger patties on the grill, and cook for 5 minutes on each side. Serve with buns, lettuce, and cucumber.

9. POTATO SALAD

Servings: 6
Preparation time: 20 minutes
Cook time: 20 minutes
Ready in: 3 hours 40 minutes

Nutrition Facts

Serving Size 294 g

Amount Per Serving

Calories 296   Calories from Fat 102

	% Daily Value*
Total Fat 11.3g	**17%**
Saturated Fat 3.0g	**15%**
Trans Fat 0.0g	
Cholesterol 91mg	**30%**
Sodium 318mg	**13%**
Potassium 983mg	**28%**
Total Carbohydrates 42.3g	**14%**
Dietary Fiber 5.1g	**20%**
Sugars 8.0g	
Protein 8.4g	

Vitamin A 23%	Vitamin C 87%
Calcium 6%	Iron 13%

Nutrition Grade B+

* Based on a 2000 calorie diet

Ingredients:

- 3 organic eggs, hard boiled and diced
- 5 red potatoes
- 3 tablespoons dill pickle relish
- 1 tablespoon prepared yellow mustard
- 1/2 onion, chopped
- 1 medium red bell pepper, diced
- 1/8 teaspoon paprika
- 1/8 teaspoon ground black pepper
- 1 cup cooked green peas

Ranch dressing:

- 1/2 cup mayonnaise
- 1/4 cup sour cream
- 1 clove garlic, crushed and chopped
- 1/4 teaspoon dried parsley
- 1 small shallot, chopped
- 1/4 teaspoon dried dill weed
- 1/8 teaspoon sea salt
- 1/8 teaspoon ground black pepper

Directions:

1. **Whisk** together the mayonnaise, sour cream, garlic, parsley, shallot, dill, salt, and pepper. Cover and refrigerate until serving.
2. **Place** the potatoes into a large pot and cover with water. Place the pot over high heat and bring to a boil. Cover and simmer over medium-low heat for about 15 to 20 minutes, or until tender. Drain and let cool completely. Peel the cooled potatoes and cut into chunks.
3. **Mix** the prepared ranch dressing, pickle relish, mustard, onion, bell pepper, paprika, and black pepper in a bowl. Toss in the eggs, potatoes, and green peas. Cover and refrigerate for at least 30 minutes before serving.

10. SHRIMP LINGUINE

Servings: 6

Preparation time: 15 minutes

Cook time: 40 minutes

Ready in: 55 minutes

Nutrition Facts

Serving Size 338 g

Amount Per Serving

Calories 441	Calories from Fat 133

% Daily Value*

Total Fat 14.8g	**23%**
Saturated Fat 3.9g	**20%**
Trans Fat 0.0g	
Cholesterol 185mg	**62%**
Sodium 351mg	**15%**
Potassium 324mg	**9%**
Total Carbohydrates 48.0g	**16%**
Dietary Fiber 3.6g	**14%**
Sugars 4.5g	
Protein 29.8g	

Vitamin A 35%	•	Vitamin C 70%
Calcium 8%	•	Iron 30%

Nutrition Grade C+

* Based on a 2000 calorie diet

Ingredients:

- 1/4 cup olive oil
- 3 cloves garlic, minced
- 1 medium green bell pepper, diced
- 4 cups diced tomatoes
- 1 cup sliced mushrooms
- 1 cup low-sodium vegetable broth
- 2 tablespoons organic butter
- Sea salt and black pepper to taste
- 1 (16 ounce) package whole grain linguine pasta
- 1 pound peeled and deveined medium shrimp
- 1 teaspoon Cajun seasoning
- 2 tablespoon chopped cilantro

Directions:

1. **Place** a large saucepan over medium heat; add 2 tablespoons of olive oil. Once oil is hot, add the garlic and sauté until lightly browned.
2. **Add** the green bell pepper, tomatoes, mushrooms, and vegetable broth. Cover and simmer for about 30 minutes, stirring frequently. Add the butter then season with salt and pepper. Remove pan from heat and cover to set aside.
3. **Cook** the pasta in a large pot of lightly-salted boiling water until al dente, about 12 minutes. Drain and set aside.
4. **Season** the shrimp with salt, pepper, and Cajun seasoning. Cook shrimp in remaining olive oil in a large skillet over medium-high heat. Cook until shrimp is pink on all sides, about 5 minutes.
5. **Add** the shrimp to the pasta sauce and toss to combine. Add the pasta and toss lightly. Garnish with cilantro to serve.

11. SESAME BEEF

Servings: 4

Preparation time: 5 minutes

Cook time: 10 minutes

Ready in: 45 minutes

Nutrition Facts

Serving Size 207 g

Amount Per Serving

Calories 454	Calories from Fat 228
	% Daily Value*
Total Fat 25.3g	**39%**
Saturated Fat 6.1g	**30%**
Trans Fat 0.0g	
Cholesterol 104mg	**35%**
Sodium 971mg	**40%**
Potassium 561mg	**16%**
Total Carbohydrates 23.5g	**8%**
Dietary Fiber 1.7g	**7%**
Sugars 20.1g	
Protein 35.2g	

Vitamin A 7%	•	Vitamin C 8%
Calcium 7%	•	Iron 20%

Nutrition Grade B-

* Based on a 2000 calorie diet

Ingredients:
- 1 pound beef tenderloin, cut into stir-fry strips
- 1/4 cup low-sodium soy sauce or coconut aminos
- 1/4 cup raw honey
- 1/4 cup olive oil
- 2 cloves garlic, minced
- 2 green onions, chopped
- 2 medium carrots, cut into 1 1/2 inch strips
- 2 tablespoons sesame seeds

Directions:
1. **Stir** together the soy sauce, honey, oil, garlic, and onions in a large bowl. Add the beef strips, cover, and marinate in the fridge for at least 30 minutes or overnight for best flavour.
2. **Heat** a wok or skillet over medium-high heat. Add the beef with marinade and cook for about 5 minutes. Transfer beef to a bowl (leaving the marinade sauce in the wok) and set aside.
3. **Cook** the carrot in the marinade sauce until crisp tender. Return the meat into the wok and add the sesame seeds; simmer for 2 minutes. Serve warm over rice or whole grain noodles.

12. BAKED TOFU PARMESAN

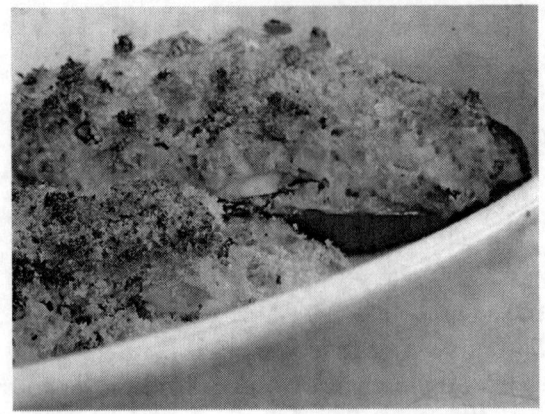

Servings: 4

Preparation time: 25 minutes

Cook time: 20 minutes

Ready in: 45 minutes

Nutrition Facts

Serving Size 232 g

Amount Per Serving

Calories 250   Calories from Fat 121

	% Daily Value*
Total Fat 13.4g	**21%**
Saturated Fat 3.1g	**16%**
Trans Fat 0.0g	
Cholesterol 8mg	**3%**
Sodium 793mg	**33%**
Potassium 419mg	**12%**
Total Carbohydrates 15.5g	**5%**
Dietary Fiber 3.2g	**13%**
Sugars 4.3g	
Protein 18.9g	

Vitamin A 20%	•	Vitamin C 11%
Calcium 30%	•	Iron 19%

Nutrition Grade B+

* Based on a 2000 calorie diet

Ingredients:

- 1 (12 ounce) package firm tofu
- 1/2 cup whole wheat bread crumbs
- 1/4 cup grated Parmesan cheese
- 2 teaspoons dried thyme, divided
- sea salt to taste
- ground black pepper to taste
- 2 tablespoons extra-virgin olive oil, plus extra for greasing
- 1 (8 ounce) can organic tomato sauce
- 1 clove garlic, minced
- 1/2 teaspoon dried basil
- 1 cup spinach leaves (cut into bite-size pieces)
- 1 cup shredded cottage cheese

Directions:

1. **Preheat** oven to 350 degrees. Lightly grease a baking sheet and an 8x8 inch baking pan with olive oil.
2. **Cut** tofu into 1/4 inch thickness. Press tofu slices with paper

towel to absorb moisture.
3. **Mix** together the bread crumbs, Parmesan cheese, 1 teaspoon thyme, salt, and black pepper in a small bowl. Coat all sides of each tofu slice with the crumb mixture then place them in the prepared baking sheet.
4. **Bake** the tofu in preheated oven for 15 minutes each side.
5. **Mix** the tomato sauce, garlic, basil, and remaining thyme; toss in the spinach. Spread half of the spinach mixture in the bottom of the prepared baking pan. Arrange tofu slices over the top. Spread remaining spinach mixture over tofu. Sprinkle with the cottage cheese on top.
6. **Bake** in preheated oven for 20 minutes at 400 degrees F (205 degrees C).

13. TUNA SALAD

Servings: 4

Ready in: 15 minutes

Nutrition Facts

Serving Size 202 g

Amount Per Serving

Calories 396   Calories from Fat 294

	% Daily Value*
Total Fat 32.7g	**50%**
Saturated Fat 5.5g	**27%**
Trans Fat 0.0g	
Cholesterol 44mg	**15%**
Sodium 361mg	**15%**
Potassium 296mg	**8%**
Total Carbohydrates 9.5g	**3%**
Dietary Fiber 5.4g	**22%**
Sugars 1.8g	
Protein 21.1g	

Vitamin A 2%	•	Vitamin C 25%
Calcium 1%	•	Iron 67%

Nutrition Grade C+

* Based on a 2000 calorie diet

Ingredients:
- 2 6-ounce cans BPA-free white meat tuna packed in water, drained and flaked
- 1/2 red onion, minced
- 1 avocado, diced
- 2 tablespoons minced celery
- 1/2 cup crushed walnuts (optional)
- 1 teaspoon minced cilantro
- 1/4 cup real mayonnaise
- 1 tablespoon whole-grain mustard
- Freshly ground black pepper, to taste
- 1 lemon, juiced

Directions:
1. **Place** the tuna, onion, avocado, celery, and walnuts in a large bowl. Stir together the cilantro, mayonnaise, mustard, pepper, and lemon in a small bowl.
2. **Add** the dressing to the tuna mixture and toss until well blended.
3. **Chill** until serving.

14. TURKEY SAUSAGE BURGERS

Servings: 2

Preparation time: 10 minutes

Cook time: 20 minutes

Ready in: 30 minutes

Nutrition Facts

Serving Size 317 g

Amount Per Serving

Calories 828 — Calories from Fat 499

% Daily Value*

Total Fat 55.5g	**85%**
Saturated Fat 23.6g	**118%**
Trans Fat 0.3g	
Cholesterol 155mg	**52%**
Sodium 1744mg	**73%**
Potassium 419mg	**12%**
Total Carbohydrates 47.4g	**16%**
Dietary Fiber 8.9g	**36%**
Sugars 8.8g	
Protein 38.4g	

Vitamin A 14%	•	Vitamin C 10%
Calcium 24%	•	Iron 20%

Nutrition Grade D

* Based on a 2000 calorie diet

Ingredients:

- 1 (8 ounce) package turkey sausage
- 2 tablespoons unsalted butter
- 2 whole grain hamburger buns split
- 4 dill pickle slices
- 2 slices cheddar cheese
- 1 small red onion, sliced
- 6 pickled jalapeno slices (optional)

Directions:

1. Divide and form the sausage into 2 patties. Fry the patties in a large skillet over medium high heat. Drain sausage on paper towels and place on a plate. Set aside.
2. Melt butter in another skillet over medium heat. Add the buns and toast until golden brown on both sides. Transfer to a plate and set aside.
3. Layer each burger in the following order: bottom bun, pickles, jalapeno slices, cooked sausage patty, cheese, onion, and top bun.

DINNER

1. ROAST STICKY CHICKEN-ROTISSERIE STYLE

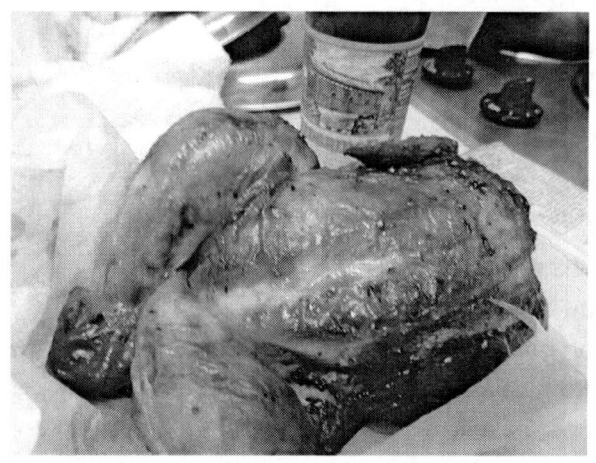

Servings: 6

Preparation time: 10 minutes

Cook time: 5 hours

Ready in: 9 hours 10 minutes

Nutrition Facts

Serving Size 317 g

Amount Per Serving

Calories 468   Calories from Fat 155

% Daily Value*

Total Fat 17.2g	**26%**
Saturated Fat 4.7g	**24%**
Trans Fat 0.0g	
Cholesterol 202mg	**67%**
Sodium 1570mg	**65%**
Potassium 692mg	**20%**
Total Carbohydrates 7.0g	**2%**
Dietary Fiber 1.4g	**5%**
Sugars 2.1g	
Protein 67.0g	

Vitamin A 12%   •   Vitamin C 12%

Calcium 5%   •   Iron 18%

Nutrition Grade B

* Based on a 2000 calorie diet

Ingredients:

- 2 teaspoons paprika
- 1 teaspoon dried marjoram
- 1 teaspoon onion powder
- 1/2 teaspoon cayenne pepper
- 4 teaspoons sea salt
- 1/2 teaspoon freshly ground black pepper
- 1 (4 pound) whole chickens, giblets removed
- 1 stick celery, cut into 3 pieces
- 5 cloves garlic, minced
- 2 onions, quartered
- 1 8-oz. can organic chicken broth
- 1 tablespoon corn starch

Directions:

1. **Combine** the paprika, marjoram, onion powder, cayenne pepper, salt, and black pepper in a small bowl.
2. **Season** each chicken inside and out with spice mixture

3. **Place** the celery, garlic, and onions in the chicken cavity. Place chickens in a re-sealable bag or double wrap with plastic wrap. Refrigerate for least 4 to 6 hours, or overnight.
4. **Preheat** oven to 250 degrees F (120 degrees C).Place chickens in a roasting pan.
5. **Bake** uncovered for 5 hours, with an internal temperature of at least 180 degrees F (85 degrees C). Let the chickens stand for 10 minutes before carving. Mix the pan drippings with the chicken broth and corn starch to make gravy.

2. VEGETABLE LASAGNA

Servings: 6

Preparation time: 25 minutes

Cook time: 1 hour

Ready in: 1 hour 40 minutes

Nutrition Facts

Serving Size 329 g

Amount Per Serving

Calories 467   Calories from Fat 197

	% Daily Value*
Total Fat 21.8g	**34%**
Saturated Fat 8.4g	**42%**
Trans Fat 0.0g	
Cholesterol 59mg	**20%**
Sodium 953mg	**40%**
Potassium 332mg	**9%**
Total Carbohydrates 46.5g	**16%**
Dietary Fiber 8.7g	**35%**
Sugars 9.2g	
Protein 24.4g	

Vitamin A 49%	•	Vitamin C 36%
Calcium 43%	•	Iron 28%

Nutrition Grade B+

* Based on a 2000 calorie diet

Ingredients:

- 1/2 (16 ounce) package whole grain lasagna noodles
- 1 tablespoon olive oil, plus extra for greasing
- 1/2 pound fresh mushrooms, sliced
- 3/4 cup chopped carrots
- 1/4 cup chopped green bell pepper
- 1/4 cup chopped onion
- 2 cloves garlic, minced
- 3 1/2 cup organic tomato pasta sauce
- 1/2 teaspoon dried basil
- 1 egg
- 1/2 (15 ounce) container part-skim ricotta cheese
- 2 cups shredded mozzarella cheese
- 2 cups chopped spinach leaves

Directions:

1. **Boil** a large pot of lightly salted water over medium high heat. Add the lasagna noodles and cook until al dente, about 10 minutes. Rinse with cold water, and drain. Cover and set aside.
2. **Heat** olive oil in a large saucepan over medium-high heat. Add the mushrooms, carrots, green bell peppers, onion, and garlic; cook until tender.
3. **Add** 2 1/2 cups of the pasta sauce and basil; stir and bring to a boil. Reduce heat to medium and simmer for 15 minutes.
4. **Beat** the egg in a large bowl. Add the ricotta cheese, 1 1/2 cups mozzarella cheese, and spinach leaves; stir to combine.
5. **Preheat** oven to 350 degrees F (175 degrees C). Grease a 9x13 inch baking dish with olive oil.
6. **Spread** the remaining pasta sauce into the bottom of the prepared baking dish. Layer 1/2 of the lasagna noodles over the sauce, and then spread 1/2 of the cheese mixture, 1/2 of the vegetable mixture, and 1/2 of the remaining mozzarella cheese. Repeat layers.
7. **Bake** for 40 minutes. Serve warm.

3. CROCK POT SPICY CILANTRO-LIME CHICKEN

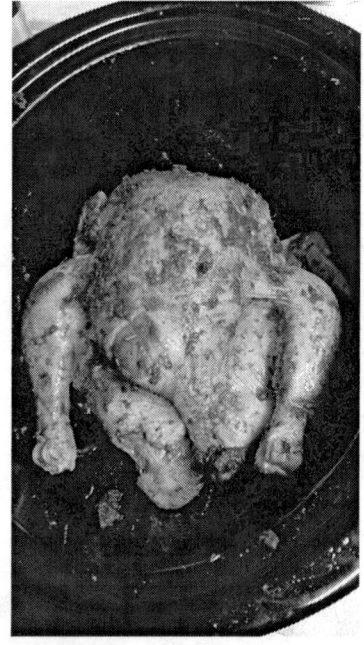

Servings: 8

Preparation time: 2 hours and 15 minutes

Cook time: 6 hours

Ready in: 6 hours and 15 minutes

Nutrition Facts

Serving Size 250 g

Amount Per Serving

Calories 457   Calories from Fat 169

% **Daily Value***

Total Fat 18.8g	**29%**
Saturated Fat 4.9g	**25%**
Cholesterol 202mg	**67%**
Sodium 440mg	**18%**
Potassium 604mg	**17%**
Total Carbohydrates 2.9g	**1%**
Dietary Fiber 0.9g	**4%**
Protein 66.0g	

Vitamin A 11%	•	Vitamin C 11%
Calcium 5%	•	Iron 17%

Nutrition Grade B

* Based on a 2000 calorie diet

Ingredients:

- 1 teaspoon black pepper
- 1 teaspoon sea salt
- 1 tablespoon chili powder
- 1 (4 pound) organic whole chicken
- 2 limes, juiced
- 2 handfuls fresh cilantro
- 3 cloves garlic, crushed
- 1 tablespoon olive oil

Directions:
1. **Mix** the pepper, salt, and chilli powder in a small bowl. Rub chicken with spice mixture and set aside.
2. **Combine** the lime juice, cilantro, garlic, and olive oil in a food processor; puree until smooth.
3. **Place** chicken and marinade in a zip-lock bag, seal, and marinate in the refrigerator for at least 30 minutes.
4. **Transfer** chicken in a 6 quart slow cooker and pour marinade over the top of the chicken,and inside the cavity.
5. **Cook** on Low for 6 to 8 hours.

4. BROWN RICE AND BLACK BEAN CASSEROLE

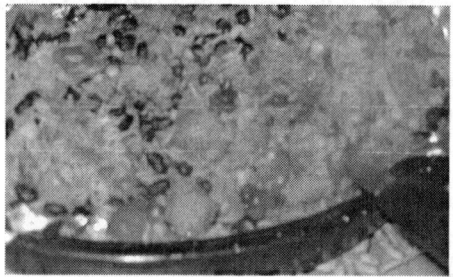

Servings: 6

Preparation time: 15 minutes

Cook time: 1 hour 35 minutes

Ready in: 1 hour and 50 minutes

Nutrition Facts

Serving Size 258 g

Amount Per Serving

Calories 533	Calories from Fat 161

% Daily Value*

Total Fat 17.8g	**27%**
Saturated Fat 9.1g	**45%**
Trans Fat 0.0g	
Cholesterol 47mg	**16%**
Sodium 536mg	**22%**
Potassium 1275mg	**36%**
Total Carbohydrates 63.7g	**21%**
Dietary Fiber 12.8g	**51%**
Sugars 3.8g	
Protein 30.7g	

Vitamin A 18%	•	Vitamin C 22%
Calcium 36%	•	Iron 29%

Nutrition Grade A-

* Based on a 2000 calorie diet

Ingredients:
- 1/3 cup brown rice

181

- 1 cup low-sodium vegetable broth
- 1 tablespoon olive oil, plus extra for greasing
- 1/2 cup diced onion
- 2 cooked skinless boneless chicken breast halves, chopped
- 1 cup shredded carrots
- 1/2 cup sliced mushrooms
- 1 teaspoon chilli powder, or to taste
- sea salt to taste
- 1 cup diced tomatoes
- 1 (15 ounce) can black beans, drained
- 1 (4 ounce) can diced green chile peppers, drained
- 2 cups shredded cheddar cheese

Directions:
1. **Place** the brown rice in a pot then cover with the vegetable broth. Bring to a boil over medium heat. Turn heat to low then cover and simmer for 45 minutes. Remove rice from heat and set aside. Place cooked rice in a large bowl and set aside.
2. **Preheat** oven to 350 degrees F (175 degrees C). Grease a large casserole dish with olive oil.
3. **Place** a skillet over medium heat, and then add the 1 tablespoon olive oil. When the oil is hot enough, add the onion and sauté until translucent.
4. **Stir** in the chicken, carrots, and mushrooms. Season with chilli powder and salt. Cook until chicken is done.
5. **Add** the cooked chicken and veggies to the rice. Toss in the tomatoes, black beans, chile pepper, and 1 cup cheddar cheese; mix well. Transfer mixture to the prepared casserole dish, and spread the remaining cheese on top. Cover the casserole loosely with foil.
6. **Bake** in the preheated oven for 30 minutes. Cook uncovered for additional 10 minutes.

5. ROASTED SWEET POTATO CORN CHOWDER

Servings: 4

Preparation time: 30 minutes

Cook time: 1 hour

Ready in: 1 hour 30 minutes

Nutrition Facts

Serving Size 460 g

Amount Per Serving

Calories 257   Calories from Fat 68

	% Daily Value*
Total Fat 7.6g	**12%**
Saturated Fat 1.1g	**6%**
Cholesterol 0mg	**0%**
Sodium 65mg	**3%**
Potassium 988mg	**28%**
Total Carbohydrates 44.2g	**15%**
Dietary Fiber 6.2g	**25%**
Sugars 4.1g	
Protein 5.4g	

Vitamin A 3%	•	Vitamin C 50%
Calcium 2%	•	Iron 15%

Nutrition Grade A-

* Based on a 2000 calorie diet

Ingredients:

- 2 sweet potatoes, peeled and cubed
- 2 tablespoons extra virgin olive oil
- Sea salt and pepper to taste
- 1 1/2 cup corn kernels
- 1 cup water
- 2 cloves garlic, chopped
- 1 1/4 cup diced red onion
- 3 cups low-sodium vegetable broth
- 1 bay leaf
- 1 potato, peeled and cubed
- 2 tablespoons chopped cilantro

Directions:

1. **Preheat** an oven to 425 degrees F (220 degrees C).
2. **Place** the sweet potatoes into a 9x13 inch baking dish, drizzle with 1 tablespoon of olive oil, toss and season with salt and pepper.
3. **Roast** sweet potatoes in the preheated oven for 15 to 20 minutes, or until tender, stirring occasionally. Set aside.
4. **Place** 1/2 cup of the corn kernels into a food processor or blender and puree with the water until smooth; set aside.
5. **Heat** the remaining olive oil in a large saucepan over medium heat. Add the garlic, and onion; sauté for 5 minutes, or until the onion is translucent.
6. **Pour** in the prepared corn puree, vegetable broth, bay leaf, and potato. Season with salt and bring to a boil over medium-high heat. Turn heat to medium-low, cover, and simmer for 25 to 35 minutes, or until the potato is tender. Discard the bay leaf.
7. **Stir** in the remaining whole corn kernels, roasted sweet potato, and cilantro. Stir and simmer until well blended.

6. HERB ROASTED PORK

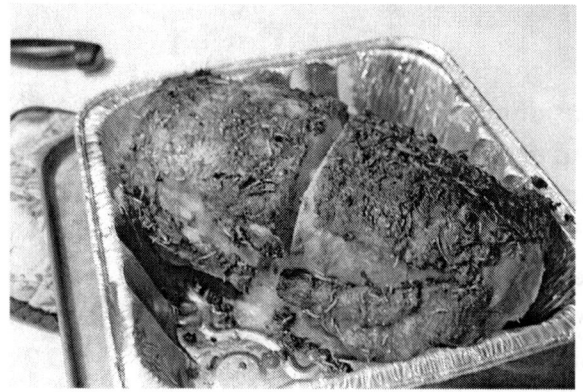

Servings: 8

Preparation time: 20 minutes

Cook time: 3 hours

Ready in: 3 hours 20 minutes

Nutrition Facts

Serving Size 284 g

Amount Per Serving

Calories 411	Calories from Fat 136

% Daily Value*

Total Fat 15.1g	**23%**
Saturated Fat 5.2g	**26%**
Trans Fat 0.0g	
Cholesterol 122mg	**41%**
Sodium 511mg	**21%**
Potassium 44mg	**1%**
Total Carbohydrates 20.7g	**7%**
Dietary Fiber 0.6g	**2%**
Sugars 18.3g	
Protein 49.1g	

Vitamin A 0%	•	Vitamin C 4%
Calcium 1%	•	Iron 2%

Nutrition Grade D

* Based on a 2000 calorie diet

Ingredients:
- 2 teaspoons dried rosemary
- 2 teaspoons rubbed sage
- 1 1/2 teaspoons olive oil
- 1/2 teaspoon sea salt
- 1/4 teaspoon ground black pepper
- 1 medium red onion, chopped
- 1 clove garlic, crushed
- 1 (4 pound) organic lean boneless pork loin
- 1/2 cup raw honey
- 1/4 cup vinegar
- 1/4 cup water
- 2 tablespoons low-sodium soy sauce
- 1 tablespoon corn starch

Directions:
1. **Preheat** oven to 325 degrees F (165 degrees C).
2. **Mix** the rosemary, sage, olive oil, salt, pepper, onion, and garlic. Cut slits in the top of the roast then rub the spice mixture all over pork. Place seasoned pork in a roasting pan on the middle oven rack.
3. **Bake** in preheated oven for about 3 hours.
4. **Mix** the honey, vinegar, water, soy sauce, and corn starch in a small saucepan over medium heat. Stir until mixture begins to thicken. Brush glaze mixture on the roast during the last 30 minutes of cooking.

7. BEEF AND VEGGIE MEATLOAF

Servings: 5

Preparation time: 10 minutes

Cook time: 1 hour

Ready in: 1 hour and 10 minutes

Nutrition Facts

Serving Size 237 g

Amount Per Serving

Calories 372   Calories from Fat 136

	% Daily Value*
Total Fat 15.2g	**23%**
Saturated Fat 4.3g	**22%**
Trans Fat 0.0g	
Cholesterol 154mg	**51%**
Sodium 237mg	**10%**
Potassium 959mg	**27%**
Total Carbohydrates 13.9g	**5%**
Dietary Fiber 2.4g	**10%**
Sugars 9.1g	
Protein 44.1g	

Vitamin A 19%	•	Vitamin C 39%
Calcium 2%	•	Iron 150%

Nutrition Grade A-

* Based on a 2000 calorie diet

Ingredients

- 2 tablespoons extra-virgin olive oil, plus extra for greasing pan
- 1 1/2 pounds lean ground beef
- sea salt and ground black pepper
- 1 cup carrots, finely chopped
- 1/2 cup red bell pepper, finely chopped
- 1 organic egg, beaten
- 1 medium red onion, finely chopped
- 3 cloves garlic, minced
- 2 teaspoons minced fresh basil
- 1/2 cup organic tomato paste
- 1 tablespoon raw honey, or unrefined brown sugar

Directions:

1. **Preheat** your oven to 350 degrees F. Grease a loaf pan lightly with olive oil.
2. **Place** the meat in a large bowl, and season with salt and pepper. Set aside.
3. **Heat** 2 tablespoons olive oil in a skillet over medium heat. Add the carrots and red bell peppers and cook until tender.
4. **Add** the cooked vegetables, egg, onion, garlic, and basil to the seasoned meat; combine well using your hands. Place the meat mixture into the prepared loaf pan.
5. **Bake** in the preheated oven for about 15 minutes.
6. **Meanwhile**, stir together the tomato paste and honey in a small bowl, then season with salt and pepper. Spread sauce on top of meatloaf. Cook for additional 40 minutes.

8. QUINOA VEGETABLE SALAD

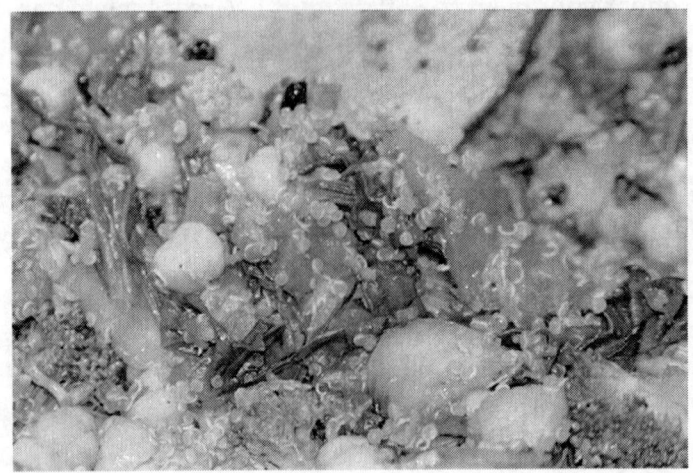

Servings: 12

Preparation time: 20 minutes

Cook time: 25 minutes

Ready in: 45 minutes

Nutrition Facts

Serving Size 259 g

Amount Per Serving

Calories 277   Calories from Fat 75

	% Daily Value*
Total Fat 8.4g	**13%**
Saturated Fat 1.1g	**6%**
Trans Fat 0.0g	
Cholesterol 0mg	**0%**
Sodium 806mg	**34%**
Potassium 554mg	**16%**
Total Carbohydrates 43.0g	**14%**
Dietary Fiber 6.3g	**25%**
Sugars 2.9g	
Protein 8.8g	

Vitamin A 22%	•	Vitamin C 54%
Calcium 7%	•	Iron 23%

Nutrition Grade A

* Based on a 2000 calorie diet

Ingredients:

- 2 tablespoons extra-virgin olive oil
- 1 tablespoon minced garlic
- 1/4 cup diced red onion
- 2 1/2 cups water
- 2 teaspoons sea salt
- 1/4 teaspoon ground black pepper
- 2 cups quinoa
- 3/4 cup diced carrots
- 3/4 cup diced fresh tomato
- 1/2 cup diced celery
- 1/2 cup diced cucumber
- 1/2 cup frozen corn kernels, thawed
- 1 medium red bell pepper
- 2 1/2 tablespoons chopped fresh basil or oregano
- sea salt and ground black pepper to taste
- 3 tablespoons balsamic vinegar

Directions:

1. **Heat** 1 1/2 tablespoons olive oil in a saucepan over medium heat. Stir in the garlic and onion, and sauté for 5 minutes, or until onion is translucent. Add the water, salt, and pepper. Bring to a boil.
2. **Turn** heat to medium-low then add the quinoa. Cover and bring to a simmer for 20 about minutes, or until the quinoa is tender. Drain the quinoa and transfer to a large mixing bowl. Chill.
3. **Add** the carrots, tomato, celery, cucumber, corn, and bell pepper to the chilled quinoa. Toss to combine and season with basil, salt, and pepper.
4. **Drizzle** the remaining olive oil and balsamic vinegar over the salad; toss well.

9. LENTILS AND SPINACH SOUP

Servings: 3

Preparation time: 10 minutes

Cook time: 55 minutes

Ready in: 1 hour 5 minutes

Nutrition Facts

Serving Size 422 g

Amount Per Serving

Calories 231   Calories from Fat 51

	% Daily Value*
Total Fat 5.6g	**9%**
Saturated Fat 0.8g	**4%**
Trans Fat 0.0g	
Cholesterol 0mg	**0%**
Sodium 731mg	**30%**
Potassium 1117mg	**32%**
Total Carbohydrates 35.0g	**12%**
Dietary Fiber 14.8g	**59%**
Sugars 6.3g	
Protein 12.3g	

Vitamin A 189%	•	Vitamin C 77%
Calcium 13%	•	Iron 33%

Nutrition Grade A

* Based on a 2000 calorie diet

Ingredients:

- 1 tablespoon extra-virgin olive oil
- 2 white onions, halved and sliced into 1/2 rings
- 3 cloves garlic, minced
- 1/2 cup lentils
- 2 cups water
- 1 (10 ounce) package frozen spinach, thawed
- 1 pinch of nutmeg
- 1 teaspoon sea salt
- 1/2 teaspoon chili powder
- freshly ground black pepper to taste
- 2 cloves garlic, crushed
- 3/4 cup finely chopped carrots
- 1/2 cup diced tomatoes

Directions:

1. **Heat** olive oil in a saucepan over medium heat. Add the onion and sauté until slightly golden, about 10 minutes.

Stir in the garlic and cook for 1 more minute.
2. **Add** the lentils, cover with the water, and bring to a boil. Reduce heat to low. Cover, and simmer to soften the lentils, about 35 minutes.
3. **Add** the spinach, nutmeg, salt, chili powder, and pepper. Simmer for about 10 minutes, stirring occasionally.

10. TUSCAN KIDNEY BEAN SOUP

Servings: 6

Preparation time: 25 minutes

Cook time: 1 hour 20 minutes

Ready in: 1 hour 45 minutes

Nutrition Facts

Serving Size 611 g

Amount Per Serving

Calories 326   Calories from Fat 145

	% Daily Value*
Total Fat 16.1g	25%
Saturated Fat 3.8g	19%
Trans Fat 0.0g	
Cholesterol 21mg	7%
Sodium 1012mg	42%
Potassium 905mg	26%
Total Carbohydrates 30.7g	10%
Dietary Fiber 9.7g	39%
Sugars 4.1g	
Protein 16.6g	

Vitamin A 103%	•	Vitamin C 55%
Calcium 12%	•	Iron 27%

Nutrition Grade A

* Based on a 2000 calorie diet

Ingredients:

- 1 cup kidney beans soaked overnight
- 3 tablespoons extra-virgin olive oil
- 1/4 pound diced nitrite-free bacon
- 2 cups diced yellow onions
- 1 cup diced zucchini
- 1 cup diced carrots
- 4 cloves garlic, sliced
- sea salt and freshly ground black pepper
- 1 1/2 cup diced tomatoes
- 1 1/2 cup chick peas, drained and rinsed
- 1 tablespoon chopped fresh thyme
- 1 tablespoon chopped fresh oregano
- 1 bay leaf
- 8 cups low-sodium chicken stock, plus extra water if needed
- 1 teaspoon red pepper flakes
- 1 (10 oz.) bag spinach leaves, cut into bite-size pieces

197

Directions:
1. **Place** the kidney beans in a medium pot, cover with enough water and bring to a boil over medium-high heat. Reduce heat to low and simmer until just-tender, about 45 minutes to 1 hour. Drain and set aside.
2. **Heat** the olive oil in a large pot over medium heat. Add the bacon and cook for 3 minutes, or until evenly browned. Drain excess fat. Stir in the onion, zucchini, carrot and garlic; sauté until tender then season with salt and pepper, to taste.
3. **Add** the diced tomatoes, chick peas, thyme, oregano, bay leaf, the cooked kidney beans, and chicken stock. Season with the red pepper flakes, salt, and pepper and simmer for about 15 to 20 minutes. Add the spinach and simmer until the beans are fully tender.

11. CHICKEN AND MUSHROOMS

Servings: 4

Preparation time: 15 minutes

Cook time: 30 minutes

Ready in: 45 minutes

Nutrition Facts

Serving Size 219 g

Amount Per Serving

Calories 245   Calories from Fat 167

	% Daily Value*
Total Fat 18.6g	**29%**
Saturated Fat 3.5g	**18%**
Trans Fat 0.0g	
Cholesterol 114mg	**38%**
Sodium 431mg	**18%**
Potassium 243mg	**7%**
Total Carbohydrates 3.4g	**1%**
Dietary Fiber 0.6g	**2%**
Sugars 1.2g	
Protein 17.9g	

Vitamin A 2%	•	Vitamin C 3%
Calcium 2%	•	Iron 13%

Nutrition Grade C

* Based on a 2000 calorie diet

Ingredients:

- 3 cups sliced mushrooms
- 4 tablespoon extra-virgin olive oil, plus extra for greasing
- 2 cloves garlic, crushed and chopped
- 4 skinless, boneless organic chicken breast halves
- 2 organic eggs, beaten
- Sea salt and ground black pepper, to taste
- 1 cup whole wheat panko bread crumbs
- 3/4 cup chicken broth
- 1 teaspoon corn starch

Directions:

1. **Preheat** oven to 350 degrees F (175 degrees C). Lightly grease a 9x13 inch baking pan with olive oil.
2. **Heat** 2 tablespoons olive oil in a skillet over medium heat. Add the mushrooms and garlic; sauté until mushroom is slightly tender. Place sautéed mushrooms in the prepared pan.
3. **Dredge** chicken into beaten eggs, and then roll in bread crumbs.
4. **Heat** remaining olive oil in skillet over medium heat. Add the chicken and brown on both sides. Arrange chicken on top of mushrooms in the pan. Mix the 1 teaspoon corn starch with 1 tablespoon water.
5. **Combine** corn starch mixture with the chicken broth and pour over the chicken and mushrooms in the pan.
6. **Bake** for 30 to 35 minutes, or until chicken is no longer pink and juices run clear.

12. STIR-FRIED TOFU WITH MUSHROOMS AND BROCCOLI

Servings: 4

Preparation time: 40 minutes

Cook time: 10 minutes

Ready in: 50 minutes

Nutrition Facts

Serving Size 258 g

Amount Per Serving

Calories 209	Calories from Fat 121

	% Daily Value*
Total Fat 13.4g	**21%**
Saturated Fat 1.6g	**8%**
Trans Fat 0.0g	
Cholesterol 0mg	**0%**
Sodium 685mg	**29%**
Potassium 437mg	**12%**
Total Carbohydrates 14.7g	**5%**
Dietary Fiber 2.4g	**10%**
Sugars 6.4g	
Protein 12.2g	

Vitamin A 6%	•	Vitamin C 74%
Calcium 18%	•	Iron 18%

Nutrition Grade A

* Based on a 2000 calorie diet

Ingredients:
- 3 tablespoons low-sodium soy sauce
- 1 tablespoon pure maple syrup
- 1 tablespoon unseasoned rice vinegar
- 1 teaspoon oriental sesame oil
- 1/4 teaspoon red pepper flakes
- 1 12-ounce package extra-firm tofu, drained, cut into 3/4-inch cubes
- 1/4 cup water
- 1 teaspoon corn starch, plus extra for dusting
- 2 tablespoons extra-virgin olive oil, divided
- 6 ounces fresh white button mushrooms, stemmed, caps quartered
- 2 cups chopped broccoli
- 4 garlic cloves, minced
- 1 tablespoon minced peeled fresh ginger
- 1 small white onion, sliced thinly

Directions:
1. **Mix** the soy sauce, maple syrup, rice vinegar, sesame oil, and red pepper flakes in a bowl. Stir in the tofu and marinate for at least 30 minutes. Drain, reserving marinade then dust tofu with corn starch. Add 1/4 cup water and 1 teaspoon corn starch to the marinade and stir.
2. **Heat** 1 tablespoon of olive oil in skillet over medium-high heat. Sauté tofu in hot oil until golden. Place the sautéed tofu in a plate and set aside.
3. **Add** the remaining olive oil to skillet. Stir in mushrooms and cook for 3 minutes, or until tender. Add the broccoli, garlic, ginger, and onion; stir-fry for 3 minutes.
4. **Return** tofu to the skillet then drizzle with the reserved marinade. Season with salt and pepper, to taste. Stir-fry until marinade begins to thicken, about 30 seconds.

13. ASIAN LETTUCE WRAPS

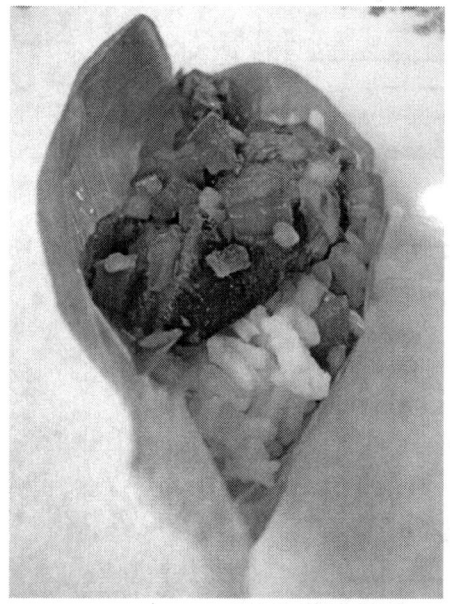

Servings: 8

Preparation time: 15 minutes

Cook time: 32 minutes

Ready in: 47 minutes

Nutrition Facts

Serving Size 229 g

Amount Per Serving

Calories 441   Calories from Fat 106

	% Daily Value*
Total Fat 11.7g	**18%**
Saturated Fat 1.9g	**9%**
Trans Fat 0.0g	
Cholesterol 58mg	**19%**
Sodium 517mg	**22%**
Potassium 405mg	**12%**
Total Carbohydrates 63.2g	**21%**
Dietary Fiber 2.2g	**9%**
Sugars 3.9g	
Protein 21.8g	

Vitamin A 11%	•	Vitamin C 19%
Calcium 5%	•	Iron 27%

Nutrition Grade B+

* Based on a 2000 calorie diet

Ingredients:

- 3 cups cooked white rice
- 2 tablespoons extra-virgin olive oil
- 1 pound ground turkey
- 1/2 cup chopped green bell pepper
- 1 teaspoon minced garlic
- 1 carrot, shredded
- 1 cup finely chopped water chestnuts
- 3 tablespoons low-sodium soy sauce
- 3 tablespoons organic hoisin sauce
- 2 teaspoons sesame oil
- 1/2 teaspoon hot chile paste
- 1/2 tablespoon cilantro, finely chopped
- 1 head butter lettuce leaves, separated
- 1 cup chopped celery
- 1 cup chopped cucumber

Directions:

1. **Heat** olive oil in a skillet over medium-high heat. Add the ground turkey, bell pepper, and garlic; cook until lightly browned, about 5 to 7 minutes.
2. **Stir** in the water chestnuts, carrot, soy sauce, and hoisin sauce, stirring frequently. Turn down heat, and stir in the sesame oil and chile paste.
3. **Fill** each lettuce leaf with a spoonful of rice and stir-fry mixture. Roll up and serve.

14. TUNA SPAGHETTI WITH SPINACH

Servings: 4

Preparation time: 5 minutes

Cook time: 10 minutes

Ready in: 15 minutes

Nutrition Facts

Serving Size 206 g

Amount Per Serving

Calories 489   Calories from Fat 133

	% Daily Value*
Total Fat 14.8g	**23%**
Saturated Fat 2.0g	**10%**
Trans Fat 0.0g	
Cholesterol 15mg	**5%**
Sodium 243mg	**10%**
Potassium 286mg	**8%**
Total Carbohydrates 67.0g	**22%**
Dietary Fiber 10.6g	**43%**
Sugars 4.0g	
Protein 24.7g	

Vitamin A 30%   •   Vitamin C 18%

Calcium 4%   •   Iron 24%

Nutrition Grade A-

* Based on a 2000 calorie diet

Ingredients:

- 350g whole grain spaghetti
- 1 small red onion, finely chopped
- 2 packed cups fresh spinach leaves (cut in small pieces)
- 85g pitted green olives, halved
- 198g can tuna in oil
- zest and juice of 1/2 lemon
- 2 tablespoons extra-virgin olive oil, divided
- 1 pinch freshly ground black pepper

Directions:

1. **Boil** the spaghetti until al dente, about 10 minutes. Drain and set aside.
2. **Heat** 1 tablespoon of olive oil in a skillet over medium heat. Add the onion and spinach and cook until spinach begins to wilt.
3. **Place** the cooked spinach and onion in a serving bowl. Add the olives, tuna, lemon zest and juice. Toss with the remaining olive oil and cooked spaghetti. Sprinkle with black pepper.

DESSERTS AND SNACKS

1. SWEET POTATO ALMOND PUDDING

Servings: 2

Ready in: 15 minutes

Nutrition Facts

Serving Size 172 g

Amount Per Serving

Calories 250   Calories from Fat 101

% Daily Value*

Total Fat 11.2g	**17%**
Saturated Fat 6.7g	**33%**
Trans Fat 0.0g	
Cholesterol 0mg	**0%**
Sodium 100mg	**4%**
Potassium 428mg	**12%**
Total Carbohydrates 38.0g	**13%**
Dietary Fiber 6.6g	**26%**
Sugars 9.9g	
Protein 5.5g	

Vitamin A 222%	•	Vitamin C 13%
Calcium 14%	•	Iron 18%

Nutrition Grade A-

* Based on a 2000 calorie diet

Ingredients:
- 1 cup mashed boiled sweet potato
- 1/4 cup almond milk
- 3 tablespoons chia seeds
- 1 teaspoon pure maple syrup or raw honey

Directions:
1. **Place** all ingredients in a food processor or blender.
2. **Blend** until a pudding consistency is reached. Chill before serving.

2. BERRY PARFAIT

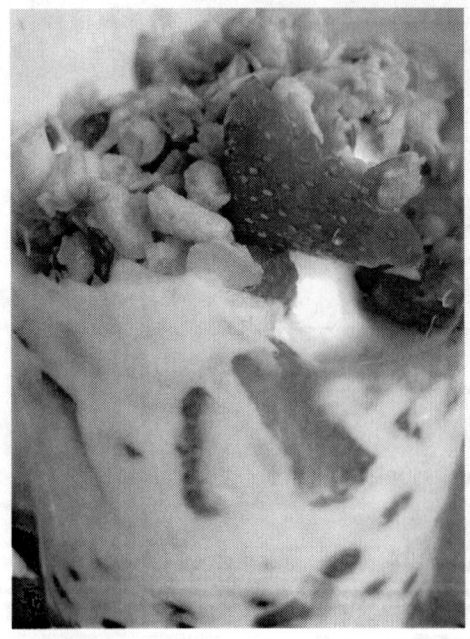

Servings: 3

Ready in: 10 minutes

Nutrition Facts

Serving Size 178 g

Amount Per Serving

Calories 226   Calories from Fat 87

	% Daily Value*
Total Fat 9.7g	**15%**
Saturated Fat 1.7g	**9%**
Trans Fat 0.0g	
Cholesterol 4mg	**1%**
Sodium 26mg	**1%**
Potassium 200mg	**6%**
Total Carbohydrates 26.8g	**9%**
Dietary Fiber 5.1g	**20%**
Sugars 21.2g	
Protein 11.5g	

Vitamin A 1%	•	Vitamin C 37%
Calcium 12%	•	Iron 8%

Nutrition Grade A-

* Based on a 2000 calorie diet

Ingredients

- 1 cup fresh blueberries
- 1/2 cup sliced fresh strawberries
- 1 cup Greek yogurt
- 2 tablespoons raw honey or pure maple syrup
- 1/2 cup chopped nuts (almonds, hazelnut, walnut)
- 1 teaspoon chopped fresh mint leaves

Directions:

1. **Combine** the berries and place them evenly in parfait glasses.
2. **Stir** together the yogurt and honey in a small bowl.
3. **Pour** yogurt mixture into each glass and top with the chopped nuts and mint.

3. AVOCADO CHOCOLATE WHIP

Servings: 3

Ready in: 20 minutes

Nutrition Facts

Serving Size 140 g

Amount Per Serving

Calories 255	Calories from Fat 128

	% Daily Value*
Total Fat 14.3g	**22%**
Saturated Fat 3.1g	**16%**
Trans Fat 0.0g	
Cholesterol 0mg	**0%**
Sodium 27mg	**1%**
Potassium 444mg	**13%**
Total Carbohydrates 33.6g	**11%**
Dietary Fiber 6.0g	**24%**
Sugars 25.3g	
Protein 3.4g	

Vitamin A 2%	•	Vitamin C 11%
Calcium 2%	•	Iron 7%

Nutrition Grade C

* Based on a 2000 calorie diet

Ingredients:

- 1 large avocado (or 2 small), peeled and pitted
- 1/4 cup raw honey or unrefined brown sugar

- 2 tablespoons unsweetened cocoa powder
- 1/2 teaspoon pure vanilla extract
- 1/2 cup soy milk

Directions:

Combine the avocado, honey, cocoa, and vanilla in a food processor or blender, and then gradually add the soy milk until smooth. Chill for at least 15 minutes before serving.

4. BANANA AND OATS COOKIE

Servings: 12

Preparation time: 15 minutes

Cook time: 20 minutes

Ready in: 1 hour 10 minutes

Nutrition Facts

Serving Size 75 g

Amount Per Serving

Calories 179	Calories from Fat 65

% Daily Value*

Total Fat 7.2g	**11%**
Saturated Fat 5.5g	**27%**
Trans Fat 0.0g	
Cholesterol 0mg	**0%**
Sodium 2mg	**0%**
Potassium 207mg	**6%**
Total Carbohydrates 27.6g	**9%**
Dietary Fiber 2.9g	**12%**
Sugars 12.6g	
Protein 2.7g	

Vitamin A 5%	Vitamin C 7%
Calcium 2%	Iron 5%

Nutrition Grade C

* Based on a 2000 calorie diet

Ingredients:
- 3 ripe bananas, mashed
- 2 1/2 cups rolled oats
- 1/3 cup raw honey
- 1/3 cup coconut oil, plus extra for greasing
- 1 teaspoon vanilla extract
- 1 cup dried fruits (such as raisins, dates, apricots, etc.)
- 1/2 teaspoon cinnamon

Directions:
1. **Preheat** oven to 325 degrees F. Grease a cookie sheet with coconut oil.
2. **Combine** all the ingredients in a large bowl then let sit for 10 minutes. Drop tablespoonfuls of the batter out onto the prepared cookie sheet; placing 2 inches apart.
3. **Bake** in preheated oven for 15 minutes.

5. BLUEBERRY BUTTERMILK PANCAKE

Servings: 4

Preparation time: 10 minutes

Cook time: 15 minutes

Ready in: 25 minutes

Nutrition Facts

Serving Size 200 g

Amount Per Serving

Calories 348	Calories from Fat 85

	% Daily Value*
Total Fat 9.4g	**14%**
Saturated Fat 6.7g	**33%**
Trans Fat 0.0g	
Cholesterol 50mg	**17%**
Sodium 531mg	**22%**
Potassium 298mg	**9%**
Total Carbohydrates 59.2g	**20%**
Dietary Fiber 2.8g	**11%**
Sugars 15.6g	
Protein 6.5g	

Vitamin A 2%	•	Vitamin C 13%
Calcium 15%	•	Iron 6%

Nutrition Grade C+

* Based on a 2000 calorie diet

Ingredients:
- 1 cup white rice flour
- 1/4 cup tapioca starch
- 2 tablespoons guar gum
- 2 tablespoons unrefined brown sugar
- 1 teaspoon baking powder
- 1 teaspoon baking soda
- 1/4 teaspoon sea salt
- 1 large egg
- 2 tablespoons coconut oil, plus more for greasing pan
- 1 1/4 cup buttermilk
- 1 1/4 cup fresh blueberries
- Maple syrup (optional)

Directions:
1. **Whisk** together the rice flour, tapioca starch, guar gum, brown sugar, baking powder, baking soda, and salt in a large bowl. In another bowl, beat together the egg, canola oil, and buttermilk until smooth.
2. **Add** the egg mixture to the flour mixture and whisk until batter is smooth. Stir in 1 cup blueberries.
3. **Grease** the bottom of a skillet with canola oil and place over medium-high heat. Ladle about 1/3 cup of batter in the skillet and sprinkle with blueberries. Cook until golden brown on both sides. Repeat with remaining batter.
4. **Serve** with maple syrup.

Conclusion

Some years back, a diabetes scare began my quest to improve my lifestyle and choose my food wisely. Since then, I discovered wonderful things about healthy eating that I wish I'd applied in my entire life. I want now to pass it down to you my readers, because anyone should have the potential to start over and achieve their dream of a healthy lifestyle.

I hope this book shed a light on your goals towards applying a successful turnout on whole foods. Now that you have good knowledge on the whole foods essentials, you should be ready and brave enough to set out strong and reach your destination.

Remember Buddha's saying, "To keep the body in good health is a duty... otherwise we shall not be able to keep our mind strong and clear."

Sincerely,

Andrea

ABOUT ANDREA HUFFINGTON

The author is a professional speaker and health coach. She works with many individuals and groups to help show them how to attain a healthy lifestyle, combining diet and a whole lifestyle plan to feel better, look better, and live better! This includes everything from helping them choose a healthy way of eating to discovering how to use "downtime" to improve their feeling of well-being.

She completed studies for a degree in chemical engineering at UCLA, where she met and married her husband James. Following that, she accepted an internship in India. Unfortunately, she was forced to return to the United States shortly after for treatment of her diabetes, which had been progressively worsening. Her health had deteriorated, and she was always tired. Like many others, she has struggled with weight problems since childhood; in addition, she has had to combat the symptoms and problems of diabetes. Also like many of us, she has tried many different diets and exercise programs, with varying degrees of success.

She began to research and try different diets in the hope of increasing her energy and feeling better. One of those diets was the Paleo diet, and since trying it, she has never looked back. There is a simple principle behind the Paleo diet. Many of the health problems we suffer from today result from a mismatch between the foods we eat and the natural diet that our bodies are meant to use. When we return to a natural diet, rich in fruits, vegetables, nuts, and natural meat, the food we eat no longer makes us sick, but rather provides us with the means to live a strong, vibrant, and energetic lifestyle. Today, the author is the picture of health and wellness, participates in triathlons and frequently gives talks on the subject of how the Paleo diet impacts sports fitness and emotional health. Her personal experiences help her audience relate to her easily, and the impact of the changes she has made gives hope to others that it can work for them as well.

Recently, she has spent three months with the San people of the Kalahari Desert, hoping to discover the secrets of their endurance and stamina in hot desert conditions. The San people hunt for their meat and forage for fruit, nuts, and roots to supplement their diet; the diet and lifestyle which they follow allows them to survive in an extremely inhospitable environment. They are thought to be the oldest inhabitants of South Africa, having been there for over 100,000 years. They have always followed a nomadic lifestyle, and have never been known to cultivate crops.

The author grew up in Southern California, and now lives in Hawaii with her husband, three children, two dogs, and a pet Boa Constrictor. She believes that keeping things simple, we can achieve so much more. This has certainly worked for her! She now concentrates on teaching and sharing with others what she has learned through research, travels, and personal experience.

BOOKS BY ANDREA HUFFINGTON

Paleo Slow Cooker Recipes

Going Paleo on a Budget

The Easy Paleo Diet Beginner's Guide

Living Gluten-free on a Budget

Paleo Pressure Cooking!

Living Gluten-free On a Budget

Before You Start...

Thank you so much for reading my book. I hope you really liked it. As you probably know, many people look at the reviews on Amazon before they decide to purchase a book. If you liked the book, could you please take a minute to leave a review with your feedback? 60 seconds is all I'm asking for, and it would mean the world to me.

Andrea Huffington

Primal Publishing

Atlanta, Georgia USA

CPSIA information can be obtained
at www.ICGtesting.com
Printed in the USA
LVOW10s1120300418
575374LV00017B/524/P

9 781499 656138